The High Middle Ages
in Germany
1000–1300

Edited by Rolf Toman

The High
Middle Ages
in Germany

Benedikt Taschen

FRONT COVER:
Calendar picture (October) from the "Très Riches Heures" of the Duke of Berry (early 15th century)
Sowing the corn

BACK COVER:
Maulbronn Monastery
Cloister

© 1990 Benedikt Taschen Verlag GmbH & Co.KG,
Hohenzollernring 53, D-5000 Köln 1
Editor: Rolf Toman, Cologne
Picture editor: Klaus Kramp, Cologne
Graphic design: Detlev Schaper, Cologne
Cover design: Peter Feierabend, Berlin
Typesetting: Utesch Satztechnik, Hamburg
Reproductions: Ceynowa & Krüger, Cologne
Printing: Druckerei Ernst Uhl, Radolfzell
Printed in Germany
ISBN 3-8228-0297-2

Contents

Introduction

For many years now there has been an astonishing interest in the Middle Ages. The popularity in Germany of exhibitions such as on the Staufer (1977) and the House of Wittelsbach (1980) and the tremendous number of books recently published on historical matters bear witness to this. Opinions differ as to the cause and depth of this interest. The publication of Umberto Eco's immensely popular mediaeval novel *The Name of the Rose* can certainly be said to have roused this interest and stimulated it, although it is doubtful whether the majority of readers would understand and appreciate the vast number of historical references in it. It is probably largely the ambience of the distant, mysterious world of the monastery and the events described that account for the fascination of this book for readers. For many people, the historical imagination needs the stimulation of the senses if it is – perhaps – to develop into an interest based on facts.

Many observers regard with suspicion this interest in the Middle Ages, in history generally, and talk of an escape into the past. They say it comes from a deep-seated need for guidance – a need which it is increasingly difficult to meet in our highly complicated world. Faced with the complexities of the present and incapable, even unwilling, to come to terms with them, many people retreat into an oversimplified view of the distant past.

There is something to this criticism, but it seems excessively pessimistic in view of the chances such a return to the past can offer. It is clear that the facts of history are not facts in an empirically scientific sense. Living as we do in the modern world we can, for example, feel gratified at our relatively high standard of living and long life expectancy compared to the hard life led by people in the Middle Ages. We may be astonished at many things our sense of rationality cannot grasp. And we are perhaps distressed that, in spite of all the progress that has been made, the loss of enchantment resulting from our rationality has left a vacuum in our senses that can, at the most, be only tolerably well concealed by a general bustle of activity. There are many ways of comparing ourselves with the past. If we pause to think for a while, we can examine the present day, our own lives, our feelings, our thoughts and the way we think in the distant mirror of the past. If we occupy ourselves with history, we thus give ourselves an opportunity to reflect – and this is an opportunity that is occasionally used.

By saying this I do not mean that history can teach us to predict future events or guide us in our actions. It would be naive to think this would be so, and anyway, this way of thinking is an extremely one-dimensional view of usefulness. But if all this talk of the opportunities of reflection offered by occupying ourselves with history is not to sound too vague, we should at least use an example here to show how historical facts can be used. But let us not forget that emotion always plays a part in our approach to historical events. During our contemplations, it is worth checking which values our emotions are related to. Let us look at the first example: our gratification or satisfaction at our relatively high standard of living and longer life expectancy. It might seem obvious to imagine one is a mediaeval peasant, crusading knight or monk and to weigh up the advantages and disadvantages of life in those days, but attempts to judge historic progress in this way get us nowhere. Can historical progress be judged at all? Is there a reasonable yardstick for comparing life in the various epochs of our history? – If, through our interest in history, we ask such questions, we have already seized the opportunities offered by reflection.

This book aims at encouraging, in an imaginative and entertaining way, an interest in historical facts and a philosophical and historic contemplation of the material. There are the many illustrations in the book to spur the reader's imagination. The text itself is both highly readable and stimulating and takes into account the fact that readers cannot be expected to know a lot about the Middle Ages. The structure of the book, illuminating everyday life in the Middle Ages and dealing with sociological, economic, political and cultural aspects, is such that it can be read as an introduction to this period. The material at our disposal is so diverse and covers such a large area that it has been deemed necessary to concentrate on the high Middle Ages (approximately the 11th to 13th centuries) and on the geographic region of the Holy Roman Empire. If, after having read the book, the reader wants to know more about the Middle Ages, there is a clearly laid-out bibliography at the end. Most of the titles, however, are in German.

In our choice of illustrations we have included work from the late Middle Ages. These illustrations are more realistic in detail than earlier work, which by comparison is cruder and more stylized. This is an important advantage, and although they are outside our period, the contents of the pictures – and this is the main thing – also tell us a lot about the period between A. D. 1000 and A. D. 1300.

Finally, thanks are due to the authors, who largely had to work without editorial co-ordination. This explains the occasional overlaps in the essays, which, however, scarcely reduce the diversity of the aspects covered. Thanks are particularly due to Mr. Klaus Kramp for his help in choosing the illustrations and writing the captions. The editor would also like to thank everybody involved in making this book.

Rolf Toman

Ways of Life in the Estates of Society in the High Middle Ages
by Tilmann Lohse

The division of mediaeval society into the three classical estates of military, clerisy and agriculture, i. e. chivalry, clergy and peasantry, is not a social order invented by historians after the Middle Ages. This division fitted the conception people of that period had of themselves and is the result of their theological view of the true order of the world. Although this outline of the social structure is only a rough one and needs some differentiation for the centuries between A. D. 500 and A. D. 1500 (the approximate dates of the Middle Ages), it is nevertheless a suitable description of society in the high Middle Ages.

Rural Life

Peasant families lived in cramped quarters – in North Germany under the same roof as the livestock, in South Germany in a different building. Conditions became even more cramped in the winter, for everybody drew closer together because of the cold. The houses were made of wood, in North Germany mainly half-timbered with wattle and daub, and the roof was either thatched with straw or rushes or covered with shingles. There were no windows and it was quite dark inside. The little light there was came in through small openings covered with a wooden grating and, in winter, stuffed with straw to keep out the cold. The floor consisted of stamped mud, the walls of rough beams or timber-work. Crude doors would be hung on leather straps or willow twigs. There was an open fireplace or, in some houses, a clay oven, with the smoke finding an outlet through the holes in the walls and doors. When it got dark, and it did so early in these windowless rooms, kindlings or tallow dips gave scanty light for working by. Burning tallow, the smell of cattle, the perspiration of the peasants themselves, the smoke from the fire and cooking – the resulting mixture of odours must have been extremely unpleasant in such cramped quarters.

The people living in these cramped conditions slept on straw mattresses either on the floor or on benches along the walls. Meals were eaten out of a wooden bowl shared by everyone sitting at a crude table. A wooden spoon, sometimes the same one for everybody, was often used, but knives were hardly necessary for there was rarely meat. Food was generally frugal and offered little variety. Since most peasant families were only able to lay in meagre stores, they were soon in danger of starvation when the harvest failed. At the beginning of the high Middle Ages the fields were still being worked with crude wheelless ploughs that only scratched the surface of the soil; the harrow was not yet in general use; the scythe with its wider sweep was only gradually superceding the sickle; and the horse collar, with which the strength of the oxen and of the tireless horses could be more efficiently utilized, was likewise only gradually becoming universal. Finally, the more productive three-field system of crop rotation was an innovation that was establishing itself but slowly. If we bear all this in mind, it becomes

The medieval estates (late 12th century)
The picture shows a medieval ruler having a nightmare: the estates rising against the king.

Medieval household equipment
Life in a peasant's home was centred on the hearth. It was here that the family met for a meal after the day's work, and it was here that warmth was to be found in the winter. The family usually ate out of a communal bowl, sometimes with everyone using just one wooden spoon. Knives were seldom necessary, for meat was rarely eaten. Cauldrons and pots, which were hung over the fire, were generally made of metal.

obvious how very dependent this peasant economy was on the weather for the success or failure of the harvest.

There were usually only two generations of a peasant family living under one roof. Death was an ever present threat. Work that sapped energy, susceptibility to disease, especially at periods of famine, and lack of medical care all led to a low life expectancy of about 40 years for the peasant population. Pregnancy was always an acute danger for the life of the mother and newborn child. The life expectancy of women, for whom a high birth rate and bad hygienic conditions were an additional risk, was even lower than that of their husbands. The rate of infant mortality was extremely high, with only 40 percent of children surviving the first years of life.

The peasant family, like all families in the Middle Ages, was patriarchal in structure. Even the arrangement of the living room made this clear. The half of the room round the table was the men's domain and the area around the hearth the women's – and this not only reflected the domestic division of labour. Peasant families consisted not only of the nuclear family but also of unmarried brothers and sisters, sometimes of more distant relatives and, on larger farms, of labourers and domestic servants. The social status of the individual members of the family depended, among other things, on the division of labour within the family. The closeness of the ties between the various members of the family depended largely on the family group being felt by everybody to be the group that organized work and livelihood. This was the only way and the only place in which survival was possible. In marked contrast to the situation today, when important functions such as making a living, part of the children's education and provision for old age have been taken outside the family, the peasant family in the Middle Ages was responsible for virtually all these aspects of life. The family grouped itself round the ownership of land. Ownership and work forced the family to stay together and also determined the form the ties took. The superior position of the man was mainly the result of his ownership of property, for the woman had generally married into his family.

The man was also in charge of the division of labour. It was he who decided on the crops to be sown and on the distribution of the harvest. It was a natural result of rural conditions that all members of the family, including very young children, had to help to the best of their ability. The men worked mainly in the fields, with the women coming to help them when necessary, such as to sow the seed and at harvest time. Thus, the women didn't merely do light work in and around the house and farmyard. For example, they sickled the corn (when the scythe started coming into use, however, it was generally the men who handled it) and bound it into sheaves; helped with the hay harvest and the threshing; tended the cattle, made the milk into butter and cheese, and slaughtered animals. On top of all this, they had to perform certain services for the lord of the manor, although to a lesser degree than the men. They had to keep a fire lit in the hearth, cook, lay in stocks, bring up the children. In spite of the patriarchal dominance of the men, women played a decisive role in the everyday life of the peasantry, which was a life in which each person was greatly dependent on the others. This mutual dependence must surely have increased the emotional ties within the family.

If we are to think our way into marital relations within the family, we must first forget our idea of marriage based on love. In those days very different factors were important in a marriage. A woman's capacity

Cutting hay with a scythe
In the Middle Ages, the scythe was used exclusively for cutting hay, never for harvesting grain. There were various types of scythe: Whether there were several grips on the handle or none at all varied from region to region. The peasant in the picture is using a scythe with two grips.

for work was of foremost importance to the man. To the parents (for it was usually they who had the task of choosing a husband or wife for their children) it was the approximate equality of possessions that influenced the choice of a partner for son or daughter. The more a peasant owned, the more important pre-marital negotiations on the material aspect were. For this reason poor peasants reached an understanding more quickly, often even without a formal marriage contract. The feudal landlord, however, had a say in the marriage contract of the peasants on his manor. If a union was in conflict with his material interests, he could veto the match or, alternatively, he could force a couple to marry. (Forced marriages decreased in the high Middle Ages). In some areas, a bondsman would have to pay his overlord a marriage fee (merchet) as payment for permission to give his daughter in marriage.

In spite of these far-reaching forms of intervention in the private life of serfs by the lord of the manor, there were areas where even he was not allowed to interfere: the peasant was his own master within the fence round his farmstead and in his own house; his house was his own domain. Here the master of the house had all the duties and rights that nowadays are regarded as belonging to the state. To this day we can find remains of this attitude tucked away in laws concerning trespass. Enclosing one's property, putting a fence round it – castles and towns

Shearing the sheep (about 1500)
Of all domestic animals, the sheep was the most widespread since it was relatively easy to keep. Sparse grassland in the lowlands provided it with grazing just as well as did the meadows of the uplands. It gave milk and cheese and, above all, wool, which was particularly important as the basic material for making clothes.

had fortified walls, and even the village as a whole was enclosed by a fence – was basic to the way of life in the Middle Ages. The fence round the farmstead was a weapon against nature in the struggle for survival. The garden and small livestock had to be protected from predatory animals and the farm animals had to be stopped from escaping and getting lost.

The enclosure provided protection and order. Units belonging together were fenced in together. The enclosure was thus a sign of growing organization. During the high Middle Ages, isolated farmsteads became increasingly rare. The peasantry were now living together with other people in villages. The revolutionary changes in agriculture taking place in the high Middle Ages went hand in hand with changes regarding the village. We now no longer assume that a settlement became a village once it had a certain number of farmsteads and people in it and that the difference between a hamlet and a village in the early Middle Ages was merely one of quantity. We now see a village as a settlement with certain features of quality – features that determine its character as a village and go beyond making it a mere collection of isolated farmsteads existing side by side. It had community amenities, such as wells, ponds, roads, regulations concerning farming, and communal organization of work. In this respect, the period of the high Middle Ages brought with it a radical change in rural life so that we can almost speak of a "villagization" of the rural population during this time. Village structures that came into being at this time shaped the life of our ancestors until well into the 19th century.

The background of this development was the amazing population growth of the time. Between the 11th and 14th centuries, the population all over Europe increased two to threefold. We have only ever seen a similar rate at the beginning of the industrial revolution. The increase in the population was strongly dependent on the rate at which land was being cultivated and exploited. New fields for growing the crops necessary for feeding the expanding population were being created by assarting woodland, draining moors and swamps and building embankments along the coasts. Advances were being made in agricultural technology, and inventions included the mouldboard plough and harrow, with the three-field system now also gaining ground. Waterpower was on the increase and the milling system expanding.

These technical innovations were accompanied by a gradual breaking up of the old system of the feudal manor. In this system, the peasant was clearly attached to the feudal manor. His relationship with his overlord or one of his deputies was very personal and close and had a great effect on the daily routine on the farm. The idea behind this system was to provide the manor with supplies. The serf (or villein) was responsible for cultivating all the fields – ploughing them, sowing the seed, reaping the corn, threshing, bringing in the harvest, guarding the harvest, grinding the corn, and also the baking. The cattle belonging to the manor had to be cared for, kept watch over and fenced in. Fence material had to be provided by the serfs. In winter, there was wood to be cut for building and burning. On top of all this, there were errands to be run and deliveries made. The serfs' wives were also included in this network of services, doing spinning, weaving, washing. The serf was required to provide his own equipment and tools, his cart, horses, oxen. There were, of course, regional differences, and feudal service was harder in some places than in others, but the principle was the same everywhere: work on the manor had absolute priority, and it was not until he had completed it that the serf was permitted to attend to his own personal matters.

The breakdown of the feudal system during the central period of the Middle Ages put an end to this concentration on the lord of the manor and his estate. The village community, the market in the nearest town with all its hustle and bustle, money – all this came into the life of the peasants. The social system changed. It was only now – with the formation of a decidedly urban population and the increasing independence of the peasantry in the 12th century – that the peasants became conscious of themselves as an estate. The feudal lord, who was now reducing his economic activity, first changed feudal service into a tax to be paid in kind, but as money became more common, payment of rent was required in the form of money. As a result, relations between the feudal lords and the bonded villeins became less personal and based only on material factors. The amount to be paid was agreed on, and a value could now be put on a manorial estate in terms of money.

Until the end of the feudal manor system, rural settlements were no more than neighbourly groups of dwellings. Certain agreements were necessary to regulate life within the settlement – family parties were celebrated together, for example, and families helped each other in cases of need – but life was generally geared to one's own land and that of the feudal lord. With the end of the feudal system, however, the neighbourhood became a political community. Social relations in the village were reorganized, the village became a self-contained legal organization. Self-government increased; a village administration came into being with its own law courts with peasants on the jury. The village community, with its highly differentiated social ties, took the place of the feudal co-operative centred on the manor house. The landlord or his deputy, who was called a Schulte, Schulze, Schultheiss or Burmester, depending on the area of Germany, remained in the village, but one was aware of his presence. The village as a whole was now fenced in, thus giving visible expression to a feeling of belonging together as a community.

The most common type of village was the nucleated village, in the middle of which was the unfenced village centre with its dwellings, stables, sheds and gardens. This village core was surrounded by a ring of open fields, each of which was divided into narrow strips. Every peasant owned one or more strips in each of these open fields. He could usually only reach his land by going over field strips belonging to other people, since paths would have been wasted land at a time of food shortage. With the three-field system of agriculture, the arable land round each village was divided into three open fields, one for winter crops, one for summer crops and one left to lie fallow. The use of each field changed annually. This system made it necessary to have rules governing the use of the fields. The village co-operative or the village headman stipulated when the seed was to be sown, when the crops were to be fenced in, when they were to be harvested and when the cattle were to be allowed onto the stubble. These fields were, in their turn, surrounded by a ring of common land. This could be used by all the peasants who had a farm as grazing pasture for their cattle and as woodland for fattening the pigs and to provide wood for building and heating. The village community was indispensable for the rural economy; here the peasants were again bound to a network of dependencies of higher importance than their farms.

A peasant feeding swine on acorns in the forest (about 1520)
The normal clothes of peasants were made of rough material. They wore a shirt, short trousers and long stockings; on top of this there was a tunic, usually fastened at the waist with a belt, no longer than knee-length so as not to get in the way while working in the fields.

The lime-tree of justice (from the "Lucerne Chronicles," 1513)
In heathen Germanic times, cultic places (barrows where ancestors were buried, springs, old trees, etc.) were chosen as places where justice could be administered. This tradition of holding court in the open air was retained long after conversion to Christianity. In villages, the place chosen for pronouncing judgement was generally a fenced-in lime tree, and this was also used as a meeting place.

In spite of the self-confidence amongst the peasantry that grew with the development of such village structures, we must not view the social structure of villages in the central period of the Middle Ages as being that of a co-operative community of equal partners. In spite of its unity, the village was clearly structured. There were not only differences between wealthy peasants who, because of the size of their fields, could afford domestic servants and farm labour, and the poor peasants running their farms alone with their families. As land came into short supply and the population increased, the full-time farmers were joined by new settlers in the village, a kind of lower class – cottagers and cottars, owners of small holdings and labourers, i. e. people owning little property. Their crofts filled the gaps between the farmsteads, or they built their own huts in rows on the edge of the village. They earned a living as labourers, tended the cattle and helped the peasants when there was a lot of work to do. Thus the village fence not only enclosed people of varying legal status, free and unfree peasants. The large-scale farmer was most likely to be able to put his surplus onto the market to convert it into money that could be invested or loaned. Others were thankful just to have enough food for the winter. Older legal differences between the peasants, which at one time had been the basis of social classes, became less and less important in the high Middle Ages. More than anything else it was now material and professional criteria that determined social rank.

In the 12th and 13th centuries, it was not only the nobility and the clergy that lived from the "surplus" production of the peasants, but also the urban population, which was increasing in number at this period. In return for his efforts, the peasant was given legal and military protection by his landlord. From the town, however, he got money, part of which he gave his landlord, part of which he was allowed to keep and spend as he wished. For many peasants the urban market meant new social contacts, but above all he could sell his produce there: field crops, vegetables, fruit, animal skins for the tanner, honey, wax – the town needed everything. And it was there that the peasant could buy equipment from specialized craftsmen. He saw unfamiliar things, got to know noise, hustle and bustle, crowds of people, wares from distant parts of the world. In the town, the peasant came into contact with a world in which work was more dynamic, more rational and in which he came to see himself as a peasant, a man from the country.

Initially, the peasantry encountered the Church in the form of the clergy. If a peasant had a clergyman as a feudal lord, it was he who received the taxes, either in the form of money or in kind. All peasants paid an ecclesiastical tithe. Apart from that, meetings between representatives of the Church and simple peasants were limited to formal occasions such as christenings and funerals. It was not until the 12th century that marriages were increasingly given the blessing of the Church. Only men took part in church services; women were refused entry. In the high Middle Ages the network of parish churches in rural areas was wide-meshed and it was sometimes a long way to the next church. Compared to nowadays, the villages were very small. When, in 1215, the Fourth Lateran Council stipulated that adult Christians should go to confession and Holy Communion once a year, it not only showed that there were enough churches for this to be feasible, but also that it could be quite an effort for this commandment to be obeyed. If, however, there was a church nearby, contacts were very close. The higher ranks of

Horse's armour and tunic of chain mail
In medieval society, knights were designated for the estate of the military. To meet their duties as warriors, they needed to be suitably equipped. Apart from a helmet, sword, lance and tunic of chain mail for the knight, armour was also necessary to protect the horse. A knight's equipment was tremendously expensive – a tunic of chain mail was worth several oxen – and it was imperative for a knight to own landed property.

the clergy, however, always remained aloof from rural life. Apart from the village square, the village church was the only gathering place in the village. The stillness and attentiveness of church services we now know was presumably not usual in those days. The church service was a place to meet and exchange news, and the parishioners would get up to walk about and chat while it was taking place. Thus, apart from the religious aspect, the church service had the function of strengthening the feeling of community within the parish.

The peasantry had little chance of climbing the social ladder. A few of the unfree peasants managed to prove themselves in war and, as knights, to rise to the ranks of the lower nobility. Others left their homes and farmsteads to build up a new existence clearing land during the development of new settlements in the East.

The Nobility

Most of us associate the Middle Ages with knights in armour, castles, tournaments, fair maidens, and chivalrous love. We are even familiar with the names of some of the knights in German mediaeval literature, such as Erec, Ywein, Parzival, to mention but a few. There are films, operas and comic strips featuring knights as their heroes. Romantic pictures of them appear in the fairy tale books of our childhood. We have far fewer images of the peasantry, although it was they, after all, who made up the majority of the population. The peasants stir our imagination to a lesser degree although the nobility and the clergy depended on their labour for a living. The nobility was hardly involved in productive work, and the luxurious life led by members of the noble classes was

based on the feudal system. The aristocratic upper classes ruled the land and, above all, the people. They used their swords to protect the masses from enemies and in return were paid ample dues. The Church, too, was permeated by this social class. The bishops came from the nobility, the abbots were aristocratic, unmarried daughters and sons of the nobility became nuns and monks.

One thing we must not do is to imagine the whole of this upper stratum as being wealthy or even stereotyped. We are dealing here with a ruling class that covered a wide range of wealth and power. There were very rich noblemen and relatively poor ones. Some were exceedingly powerful, others much less so. Their legal status, too, pointed to big differences in rank. Mediaeval nobility could be roughly divided into the following hierarchy: the king was followed by the princely nobility, then came the non-princely nobility and then, on the lowest level, the *ministeriales.*

Nobleman and lady playing chess (Grosse Heidelberger Liederhandschrift, early 14th century)
In about the middle of the 12th century, the French ideal of the courtly knight started to become popular in Germany. The courtly knight was supposed to be just, brave and wise; he was also expected to be well-mannered and his behaviour towards women marked by the genteel etiquette of court.

Knights fighting (miniature from the "Jungfrauenspiegel," late 12th century)
Knights generally fought according to a fixed ritual. There was jousting at the beginning, followed by a fight using swords. The picture clearly shows the main components of a knight's armour – helmet, suit of armour, tunic, sword and shield.

A look at the development of the *ministeriales* and knighthood can tell us a lot about the social mobility of the upper stratum of mediaeval society. In the first instance, being a knight meant fighting on horseback. The necessary arms were lavish and expensive. A horse had the same value as five to ten oxen, and the armour was worth many times that. A knight going into battle took several horses with him. The horse ridden by the knight to the scene of battle was tired by the time it got there and had to be exchanged for another one, and there was a third horse carrying all the necessary equipment. This included a firm saddle as well as a helmet and sword. After A. D. 900, stirrups gave fighters on horseback a firm hold while jousting. A man wanting to be a knight had to own property if he was to be able to afford such an expensive outfit.

If the upper nobility was to be militarily strong and powerful as a dynasty, it was necessary to recruit fighters from the lower classes. For free-born thanes, or "Edelfreie," and, increasingly frequently, non-aristocrats and bondsmen, this was an opportunity for social advancement. It was this group of people that formed the class of *ministeriales*. In the early Middle Ages, the peasantry had been able to supply the militiamen needed. But now, as feuds within the upper stratum increased, the nobility had to have a permanent military power at its disposal. The peasants – free peasants with a little landed property – who had hitherto been used for military purposes, were gradually being ruined by frequent war service since their fields were continually being left uncultivated. The weaker of them became serfs. Others, however, who managed to hold their own, were granted a fief, found a future in knighthood and climbed to the ranks of the lower nobility as vassals.

There is another line of development that is important for growing differences within the social structure of the nobility in the high Middle Ages. The gradual establishment of territorial states by the upper nobility, the rapid population growth and the extensive expansion and differentiation of the economy called for a change in the structure of the administration by the ruling class. As in the early Middle Ages, there were not enough free vassals available for all the new tasks. Princes of church and state alike were thus increasingly dependent on serfs, both for their administration and their wars. The members of the new class of social climbers, the *ministeriales*, needed to be well provided with material goods if they were to be able to attend to their chivalrous services. The *ministeriales* needed landed property and subordinate peasants. The landed property provided by the feudal lords became inheritable (and thus personal property) during the 11th century and was the basis of the advance of the *ministeriales* to the ranks of the lower nobility.

Apart from war service, the *ministeriales* were responsible for the landlord's own economy. They not only supervised the peasants and craftsmen in bondage in the manorial undertakings (miller, baker, blacksmith, forester, brewer, huntsman) but also the merchants in bondage. This was a time of castle building, and during this period the *ministeriales* became castle bailiffs and burgraves. Thus they reached positions above the mass of serfs.

This position between the lowest classes and the upper stratum was the beginning of many a career. It was also the beginning of a new aristocratic class. The *ministeriales* furthermore took on administrative tasks for the princely nobility. Important sections of the territorial nobility came from this class of social climbers. One-time servants became important functionaries. They increased their power and sometimes became equal with the old nobility.

The opportunities for the *ministeriales* to become rich were good in the towns. Here they took part in long-distance trading and accumulated wealth. Once they had reached a strong social and economic position, it was almost a matter of course for them to change their legal position as serfs. It seems to have been of advantage to be a *ministerialis*, for there were even cases of free noblemen voluntarily taking on this servile rank. During the High Middle Ages in Germany, the nobility had not yet started to shun contacts with lower classes as they did in the later Middle Ages, when the *ministeriales* belonged to the nobility.

The *ministeriales* owed their rise to the fact that they were needed as ruling instruments by the kings and upper nobility to establish or to expand and protect territories of rule. There were, of course, big social differences within the *ministeriales* group, and these were largely related to the power held by their overlords. But a social rise always resulted in imitations, and so a common way of life came into being that was geared to the example of the upper nobility. In this way, a kind of courtly culture came into being, although the aristocratic reality was seldom as splendid as the picture painted by mediaeval literature. It was not long before the life led by the old nobility was indistinguishable from that of the *ministeriales*. In the 13th century a lot of old noble families died out and the *ministeriales* formed an increasingly large proportion of the upper stratum. By about 1300, the *ministeriales* accounted for some 80 percent of the nobility. At about this period, amazing radical social changes and shifts of power were taking place.

Socially, the *ministeriales* was the class from which chivalry drew its strength. For the *ministeriales*, knighthood was a vehicle for social rise. There were free vassals among the knights, but by far the greatest number of them were *ministeriales*. Knighthood as a concept was not just tied to this social class. It was central to aristocratic culture, and it also united the virtues and ideals of the nobility's way of life as well as the way it thought of and saw itself. It may, therefore, seem all the more amazing that "knight" as a class term later referred mainly to the lower nobility.

Calendar pictures (January to December) from the "Très Riches Heures" of the Duke of Berry (early 15th century)
The following 12 pages are from one of the most beautiful and famous books of hours of the Middle Ages, the "Très Riches Heures" of the French Duke of Berry (1340–1416). It consists of pictures for the months of the calendar at the beginning of each of the books of hours, since the user of this liturgical book had to know which prayers were to be said on which day, whether the day in question was a working day or a holy day and which saint was to be honoured. Over each of the pictures, which show work typical of the nobility or the peasantry, there are semi-circles containing astronomical information.
January: Duke of Berry's New Year reception
February: Winter on the farm
March: Peasants working fields, ploughing and pruning the vines
April: Wedding scene of the nobility
May: Nobility out riding
June: Peasants making hay
July: Harvest and sheepshearing
August: Falconry
September: Grape picking
October: Sowing the corn
November: Collecting acorns for swine
December: Boar hunting

What was it that was so typical of chivalry as such? What did knights have in common? From a material point of view, they were wealthy enough to afford a lifestyle that left them free to go to battle. Most of them were young, and their behaviour was greatly influenced by a certain ideal of masculinity. The thing was to be unmarried, impetuous, plucky and belligerent. Training in the art of war took years. The first two to four years of the training were those of the junker (i. e. "Jungherr" = young gentleman). At the age of 14, the apprentice knight became a squire at court and then, at the age of 20, a fully fledged knight. Not all the junkers managed to reach their goal of knighthood, for not everyone was in the necessary physical condition. The training of a knight was concluded by an accolade, a ceremony during which the weapons were handed over and the nobleman knighted. This was followed by several days of festivities – expensive, colourful, wild, with tournaments. Afterwards it was up to the young knight to prove himself in battle, to have adventures and go looting. This kind of life required courage, daring and strength. A knight's reputation depended on his victories, and this is what he strove for. He was not interested in book learning. Chivalrous fighting was above all a ritualized duel and included using lance and sword. Long-range weapons were regarded as being unchivalrous. Even a battle was fought according to certain rules. The time and place were agreed upon, and ambushes and other tricks were not in keeping with chivalrous honour. Such conventions certainly seem plausible if we bear in mind the effort and time necessary for a knight to get into his full outfit. And yet we must be careful not to equate the rules of fighting as we know them from epics of chivalry with the reality of war. If the worse came to the worst, brutal, unrestrained violence is more likely to have been the rule. The state did not monopolize the right to violence in those days, and no one seems to have been particularly bothered about authorizing the use of force. The fact that the literature of the day kept stressing the need for discipline and moderation could be an indication that in reality these chivalrous ideals were in a bad way. Knights could be excessively violent, uncontrolled while fighting (especially in battle against someone of lower rank), rough with women (which is a contradiction of the image we have of knights paying homage to fair maidens). This is why we so often find attempts in literature to curb the impetuosity and wildness of knights by praising high ideals, the message being that knights should at all times protect honour and show loyalty, justice, good nature and a kindly manner – all virtues intended to check the passions of this estate. This is also how we should understand its task of protecting the Christian faith. The knight was expected to use his energy to serve the poor and helpless – charitable conceptions that inspired the Knights of Malta, the Templars and the Teutonic Order of Knights.

The Age of Chivalry was also a period associated with castles. A lot of castles were built during the high Middle Ages – so many, in fact, that we can almost say it was the policy of the nobility. Aristocratic castles were an expression of the power of large families and were ruling instruments, not only symbolically but in actual fact. They were administered by *ministeriales*, built by villeins in thousands of days of service for the feudal lord in three to seven years. Their most important function, still clearly visible today, was that of defence. The opponent was conquered once his castle had been taken. That is why castles were on such inaccessible hills – that is why their walls were so thick and high. They were also often used as prisons (as indeed monasteries sometimes

Eltz Castle (first documented mid-12th century) In Germany, only the kings originally had the privilege of being allowed to build fortifications to repel intruders. Punishment for building a castle without permission was severe. It was not until the 11th century that the nobility started fortifying their homes. Eltz Castle (on the River Mosel) was a coparcenary castle, i. e. through inheritance it had become the common possession of several noblemen.

The Prince of the World (Strasbourg minster, c. 1275)
Clothing had always been a special sign of one's social status and was an outward mark of power and affluence. Typical of the clothes of the nobility in the 12th and 13th centuries were, above all, the bright colours of the valuable materials, clearly setting them apart from the simple greyish-blue or black tunics worn by peasants.

were). The area within their walls was under the castellan's jurisdiction. The castle was the centre of the manor of the feudal lord – the centre of his administration, so to speak, and at the same time a stately meeting place for the nobility. It was a widely visible sign of his rule, outwardly fortified, repellent for peasants in their wooden huts, threatening, monstrous, built in stone for eternity. This is expressed by the castle sites – set apart from the settlements, on hills, at a distance from the ruler's subjects. The keep, towering 20 to 30 meters above the already high castle building, was a special status symbol in this male-dominated world; it was also a refuge if the castle walls were ever surmounted by the enemy.

Luxury goods were sold within the castle walls, brought by merchants from distant parts – exotic spices (which were expensive and popular in the Middle Ages), valuable cloths in the brightest of colours, elaborate tapestries and all sorts of other things. This is where courtly festivals were held, centred on the banquet. A crowd of servants waited on the assembled company in the great hall. Minstrels entertained the guests, music and poetry were performed, actors and acrobats displayed their arts. It was here that the *minnesang* – poetry recited in public – found a suitable social framework. Festivities sometimes went on for days, although this did not happen very often, as the cost was immense. And by no means all the lords of the castle could afford such festivities, much as they would have enjoyed the social prestige they brought. Castles were often also the setting for tournaments; these were both military exercises and sport, giving knighthood an opportunity to show itself off. The tournaments were fought according to set rules. Although blunt weapons were used, a lot of people were injured and sometimes even killed. At the beginning of such tournaments there were exhibition fights between groups, followed by jousting in pairs on horseback, and then finally fighting with swords until one of the swordsmen gave up. It was the climax in the life of a knight to win a tournament at a big festival. But such climaxes were few and far between. A knight's daily routine was dominated by other duties and the normal life of a knight was anything but glamorous.

Monastic Life

The Middle Ages are always and rightly called Christian – and yet this is relative, for Christianity did not come to the majority of European countries until during the Middle Ages, and northern Europe was not nominally converted until as late as the 11th and 12th centuries. Little is known about the extent to which Christian thought shaped the daily routine of the majority of people. Literary sources of this period could give a misleading impression, since writing was for a long time mainly limited to monastic life. Religious life in the monasteries, the strongholds of the practical aspect of Christianity, is well documented, and the way we see the Christian Middle Ages is largely influenced by the effects of monastic culture.

Christianity in the Middle Ages did not establish itself from below, as in early Christian conversion, when each convert had made his own decision, but was imposed on the people from above after the political leaders, those in power, had decided to become Christian. The Christianized country was then given a network of parish churches with collecting places for tithes. Within the German empire, this process had more or less been completed by the high Middle Ages. Christianization by no means meant that religious practice was the same everywhere. Rather it can be assumed that old, often local, religious traditions formed the basis for the new religion without, however, becoming completely ineffectual in the process.

People in the Middle Ages felt continually threatened, at the mercy of the power of nature, helpless in the face of hunger after failed harvests, of epidemics and raids by armed marauders. It is hardly surprising that they turned to religion as medicine for the soul. But belief brought anything but peace of mind. Religion itself contained terrifying elements. After all, was not Doomsday expected to come in the year 1033, 1,000 years after the crucifixion of Christ? That year of all years, there happened to be an eclipse of the sun, causing dread and panic. Death was omnipresent in the Middle Ages; it came earlier than it does nowadays, and it often came unexpectedly. It was rare for people to achieve peace and security. This might have been one of the reasons for them to move closer together, in villages and towns. The community of the village and the strong, fortified walls round the town had a comforting effect on the menaced people – action was being taken against the danger, alliances being made. The co-operative aspects of the village community will not only have been seen from a pragmatic point of view: apart from such things as jointly paying for the services of someone to tend the animals, the aim was to create a sense of community and security.

If there was danger from without, the feudal lords and knights were responsible for protecting their subjects. It was this task of protecting the community that justified the existence of the feudal system – protection in return for the dues paid. And it was the clergy who were in charge of

Cistercian monks working in the fields (12th century)
As a reaction to the increasing "worldliness" of monastic communities there came into being in the 12th century numerous reform orders that particularly emphasized the ideal of poverty, following the example of Jesus Christ. The Cistercians took the principle of "ora et labora" especially seriously. The oldest statutes of Cîteaux say, "The monks in our order must live from the work of their hands, cultivating the land and breeding animals".

Dominicans at Divine Office
At the beginning of the 13th century, Dominicus, with the encouragement of Pope Innocent II, founded an order that was particularly concerned with preaching the gospel and set new standards in this field. The Dominican order played an important role in the development of scholastic philosophy and opposition to heresies. The most famous inquisitor in the Middle Ages, Bernardus Gui (d. 1331), was a member of this order.

spiritual well-being and had to take the responsibility for spiritual anguish. The people felt the anguish to be so dreadful that their own prayers were apparently not sufficient. It is virtually impossible for us to imagine the tremendous fear, a fear that could be physically felt, that used to torture mediaeval people – and let us not forget that, after all, they believed in the literal existence of the devil. These fears called for a priest, whose most important task was to care for the spiritual welfare of the people, and monks living in monasteries, where they prayed for the salvation and welfare of the world. Let us now concentrate on the monasteries, which, in the Middle Ages, had numerous connections to the world outside and the cultural significance of which as a whole cannot be too highly stressed.

Presents of land very early in the Middle Ages had given some monasteries manorial power. The influence of the monasteries on mediaeval society was thus by no means merely cultural and religious in character, but also political and economic. Peasants had to perform feudal services for monasteries, and paid dues in the form of produce and taxes as well as church tithes if the monastery was the parish church. Thus the monastery in Prünn in the duchy of Upper Lorraine (which in those days was part of the German Empire) had a total of 2,000 *Hufen* (crofts) with corresponding obligations towards the monastery, as well as 35 mills, seven breweries and woods with 6,700 fattening pigs. The peasants on this particular manorial estate performed 70,000 days of service for their feudal lord, transported 4,000 cartloads of goods, and provided 2,000 quintals of grain, 4,000 chickens, 1,800 pigs and 4,000 buckets of wine. These figures make it clear what economic power monasteries could have. And apart from the manorial estate, there were also holdings belonging to the monastery and run by lay brothers. Monasteries that were economically less powerful aimed at least to be self-sufficient, and surplus in production was sold. Apart from agriculture, a lot of the monasteries had their own commercial businesses.

The path to becoming a monk was usually long and not open to everyone. The mediaeval idea of the ages of man stipulated that childhood ended with the seventh year of life. For most people this early entry into the world of adults meant working on the fields or in a craftsman's business. Noble families, too, made important decisions for the future education of their children at the age of seven. To prevent the estate being divided, a lot of children were committed to the care of a monastery, and handicapped children were often also destined for life in a monastery. Since it was common for novices to be accepted by monasteries only if the family made a donation, the monasteries were inhabited exclusively by members of the nobility, for who else but they was able to fulfil this condition! Thus the church and the nobility formed a single social unit; the clergy and monks were of noble stock, bishops and abbots came from powerful and well-known families.

The seven-year-old "child oblates" *(pueri oblati)* had to submit to strict discipline at a very early age. They were under the permanent control of a teaching monk. For example, they had to sit apart from each other and were not allowed to talk or communicate with one another, let alone touch each other. The teaching monk was always present, even when the boys were washing or going to the toilet. This training and discipline lasted until the age of 15, and then came the noviciate. At the age of about 16, novices would take the vows of poverty, chastity and obedience, thus closing the doors to the outside world for ever, for they

The Benedictine monastery of Saint Martin-du-Canigou
The monasteries in the Middle Ages had various functions. They were not only focal points of religion and the cultivation of belief, on the one hand, and of culture and education, on the other; they were also extremely important economic centres. The Benedictines and the Cistercians in particular played a significant role as technical innovators.

Tombstone of Archbishop Siegfried III of Eppstein in Mainz cathedral (c. 1249)
In the Middle Ages, members of the nobility without their own source of income were often appointed to vacant bishoprics, since the bishops not only possessed great authority, for example as city lords, but also because on a supraregional level they were a political factor of the first degree. Thus, the archbishops of Mainz, Trier and Cologne could take part in the election of the German emperor and therefore exerted great influence on imperial politics.

were normally tied to this particular monastery for the rest of their lives. The rank of the monks within the monastery was determined among other things by their "professed age," i. e. the number of years since vows were taken. The younger monks gave precedence to the older ones; the older men were called "nonus" (grandfather) and the younger monks "frater" (brother). This was the order for the seating arrangements in choir and the order in which Holy Communion was taken. There were also other criteria, and these could alter the order laid down by the professed age or possibly even nullify it. Promotion or demotion was possible to reward or punish monks for their way of life. The different offices and tasks in the monastery enjoyed varying degrees of repute and power, and the offices each monk had assumed were even more decisive. It was also important what sort of family the monk came from. The more powerful the monk's family was in the outside world, the greater the chances for the monk usually were to take over important positions and to grow in repute within the monastery walls.

The monastery was headed by the abbot, and he had to be obeyed by all the monks. The abbot's power was not just limited to life within the monastery, but also involved representational tasks outside. The powerful abbot was assisted by his deputy, the dean, who also had the task of representing the interests of the brothers to the abbot. Then came the provost. His job was the administration of the monastery as an economic enterprise: the monastery's own land, the manorial estate and other property. Larger monasteries sometimes had several provosts. The cellarer managed equipment, clothes, stores. He was also in charge of the kitchen. This office was sometimes divided, with clothes and cattle being placed in the hands of the chamberlain. The relief of the most immediate needs of the poor and sick was regarded by the monasteries as being their Christian duty, and it was the hospitaller who looked after them. The gatekeeper, or porter, had a cell of his own at the entrance to the monastery. Other of his duties included the care of liturgical utensils and vestments and ringing the bells, which, in view of the monks' precisely regulated daily routine, was important. The monks' daily routine was far too complicated for them to do as the rural population did, namely to keep time by following natural events like daybreak, the height of the sun at midday and sunset. As a result, increasingly better ways of measuring time were developed in the monasteries. One extremely important position was that of the librarian, who was often also the teacher of the "child oblates." After taking their vows, young brothers generally started their monastic careers as writers of documents, copiers, illuminators. A brother who did these jobs well had good chances of going far in his career as a monk. Older, experienced monks were sent as messengers to other monasteries, to the bishop, the king or even the pope, or they were priests in the monasteries' own church. A lot of these offices show that the monasteries had more or less direct contact with the outside world even if the monks themselves, with the exception of messengers, never went outside the monastery walls for the rest of their lives.

The monks' daily routine was something like this. The day began early. At one o'clock in the morning, after four hours' sleep by candlelight in a communal dormitory and without undressing, they rose to celebrate mass. Mass was followed by morning prayers at daybreak. Since they had had so little sleep, it was quite possible that someone would fall asleep during the day. This was regarded as being a particularly bad crime, especially if it happened during choral singing. Between hourly prayers in the morning and afternoon, there were periods set aside for work, which for monks from aristocratic families was mainly intellectual. The monks' duties included writing and studying the Bible – apart from a very few exceptions, they were for centuries the only people who could read and write. Monks who held office also performed their own special tasks during this time. In the high Middle Ages physical work was generally done by laymen. Meals were eaten in a communal refectory; the main meal was at twelve o'clock, but during periods of fasting it was not served until the evening. Food was plentiful and varied, as can be seen from the accounts. Meals were even more sumptuous on feast-days.

Looked at from a modern point of view, monastery life was rather unhealthy – unlike knights, monks were not allowed to live out their emotions sufficiently. However, hygiene was taken very seriously. The rule prescribed a daily wash, on Saturdays the whole body and at Christmas and Easter a bath – which was a lot for those days. There were rules governing everything; even a visit to the lavatory was to take place at set times.

The monasteries not only made agricultural produce, they also processed it. They had their own mills, bakeries and, above all, breweries, some of which are still famous today, for example those in South

Ground plan of St. Gallen monastery (early 9th century)
None of the medieval monastery layouts have been completely preserved; this makes the St. Gallen monastery plan all the more important. However, it does not represent an actual building but was an ideal layout of a monastery. The entire layout covers an area of 145 x 205 metres. In the centre there is the church and the monks' cells.

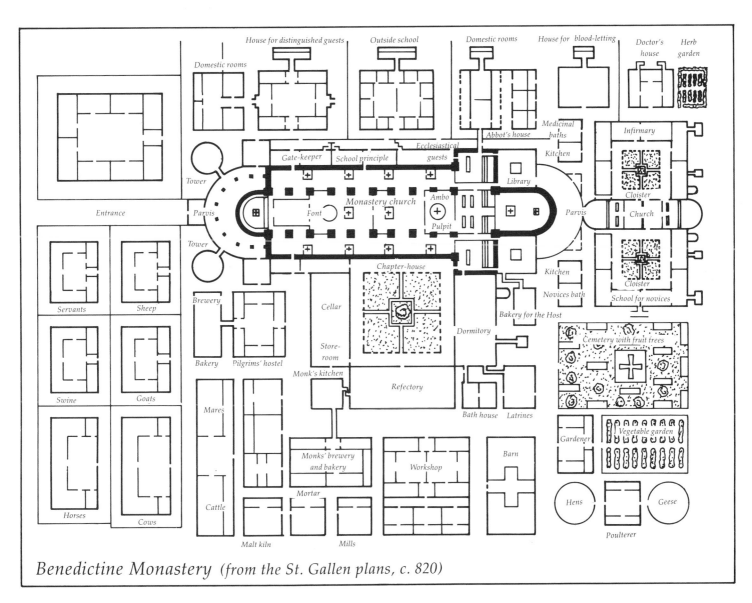

Benedictine Monastery (from the St. Gallen plans, c. 820)

Monk and pupil
In the Middle Ages, the monasteries were the most important and, initially, the only places of education. In the so-called "inner schools," the child oblates, i. e. boys intended for the life of a monk, were prepared for their monastic existence, while the education of clerics and secular priests took place in the "outer schools." It was not until the 12th century that it became common for princes to entrust their sons to monastery or cathedral schools without intending them to embark on a "career" as monks. Very often, too, the education of the sons of the nobility was placed in the hands of private tutors.

Germany. It was not the monks who did the work in these various enterprises, but lay brothers living in a separate part of the monastery from the monks, assisted by bondsman peasants and craftsmen. These lay brothers led a life of their own in their own community, had their own part of the church and were the monks' servants and workers. They cultivated the fields, tended the cattle, looked after the sick, were craftsmen and merchants. They were dressed differently from the monks, according to their position within the hierarchy and their work. In this way monasteries reflected the mediaeval idea that society was divided according to whether people did physical work or not.

The bondsmen paid their dues to the monasteries and had to perform feudal services there. But they also learnt the techniques and skills used by the lay brothers in the garden and crafts shops. Trading between the monasteries and towns increased noticeably. On the one hand, the monasteries sold their surplus agricultural produce at market in the towns, and on the other hand merchants from the towns went to the monasteries. Here the townsfolk came into contact with new inventions and know-how and received new incentives for their own activities. The provost sometimes visited distant estates, where he would give instructions involving the use of the latest knowledge. During this period monasteries had an important influence as economic enterprises. And new economic forms caused social change. The Cistercians in particular, who, compared to the Benedictine monks, consciously devoted more of their time and energies to productive work, played a decisive part in creating and spreading new inventions. They were responsible for the introduction of the three-field crop system in large parts of Germany; they invented the use of water power and improved the smelting of iron ore. The division of labour in their own enterprises was modern in our sense of the term. They had running water in their monasteries, directed along lead or wooden pipes to the workshops. Their gardens, too, were irrigated with the help of water pipes, and they had flush lavatories. They used new systems of ditches to drain marshy land, and dug channels to supply mills with water. All these innovations, and many others besides, had an influence that must not be underestimated. Completely new professions and occupations came into being – the list of skilled trades in the towns is very long. All these new developments brought changes in social structure, for some people became specialists and others were dependent on them; on the whole, people grew increasingly dependent on one another, and new social groups and positions in the hierarchy came into being. And it was the monasteries that were largely responsible for these developments. Seclusion was only one aspect of monastery life, for it was often anything but complete: technological and economic contacts were made with the outside world, roads and bridges were built, monasteries were involved in new regions being opened up and exploited and in clearing land and forests. On top of all this, the monasteries played a decisive role in developing the sciences, theology and philosophy. Antique scripts were copied and studied in the scriptoria and the works of the church fathers carefully worked through. Monks wrote their own scripts – monastery chronicles, biographies of the saints, accounts of miracles. Monks gifted in painting illustrated the books with the miniatures we still admire today. The monasteries were the cultural centres of the period. Apart from this culture, however, there was also the lay culture of the Middle Ages – that of the court and chivalry.

There was no such thing as social welfare in the Middle Ages. But there were certainly plenty of old people, sick people, and cripples who had no hope of providing for themselves and lacked a family to look after them. Here the monasteries had a function that was very much in the public interest and which had a direct influence on society. The monks felt they were responsible for charity and welfare. The poor were fed on certain days, occasionally bathed, shaved and even clothed. There were sometimes hundreds of people to be dealt with, a figure that not only tells us a lot about the wealth of the monasteries, but also gives us an idea of the size of the problem of poverty at the time. Then we must not forget that in those days there were no guest houses or inns, so monasteries were the only place for travellers to spend the night. Monasteries were essential to travel in the Middle Ages. In some monasteries there were alms houses which were also used as hospitals. In this way part of the dues paid by the serfs flowed back to the poorest strata of society.

Monasteries were founded by kings and bishops. There were also monasteries established by members of the nobility. These were intended for unmarried sons and daughters, but they also had a pious although not selfless aim: the monks were required to pray for the soul of the deceased founders. The social reputation of a family was greatly enhanced by the ownership of a family monastery. Thus there were close ties between monasteries and the nobility. But the aristocracy also stood to gain materially by founding monasteries. The lord of the monastery (the founder or his successor) and his entire retinue were to be given hospitality while travelling through the locality; the monks dealt with his correspondence; cloister vassals had to serve in the founder's army.

The emergence of mendicant orders and their rapid rate of growth in the 13th century indicates a change in the monastic system which needs to be seen in the context of other radical changes of the time. In spite of all the interaction between monasteries and society as a whole, the monks wanted to remain cut off from the rest of the world, their aim being a secluded, chaste life without possessions. And yet the monasteries grew more and more powerful and became propertied orders. Although the monks forfeited all their personal possessions, they nevertheless belonged to the ruling class in the same way that the nobility did. By consciously dissociating themselves from these propertied orders, the begging monks grew to become a new force in the 13th century. The Franciscans were particularly important. They started off in the year 1210 with just 12 members, and only 50 years later they numbered 17,500. The brethren of this reformatory order were no longer tied to one particular place or monastery. They no longer cut themselves off from the rest of the world; they wanted no property, neither did they want their own production workshops. Their houses were open, and membership of the order was not restricted to the nobility, but included all social classes. The mendicant friars lived and worked in the towns, with donations forming the basis of their livelihood. They took the ideal of poverty very seriously, interpreting it as covering not just personal possessions, but applying to possessions held by the entire order. The Franciscans and other reformatory orders found that their main field of work, increasingly centred on the sermon, was in the rapidly growing and newly established towns. This change in the system of orders clearly indicates the radical changes taking place during this period, with the societal focus shifting from the nobility and rural life to the towns and townspeople.

Abbot and novice (Grosse Heidelberger Liederhandschrift, early 14th century)
There were generally two reasons for voluntarily entering a monastery – calling or concern for the salvation of one's soul. As a rule, however, the monks had had little choice about entering a monastery, since they had been entrusted to the strict upbringing of a monastic order while still children. As admission to a monastery was associated with a gift, it was really only the landed nobility who were able to choose the life of a monk. As a result of this practice, the monasteries were increasingly limited to the nobility.

Monarchy and Nobility:
On the Delicate Balance of Power in the Middle Ages
by Ludwig Vones

Equestrian statue of Charlemagne (9th century)
By far the most remarkable ruler in the early Middle Ages was Charlemagne (742–814). After his coronation as king in 768 (he was proclaimed emperor in 800), he resolutely and successfully pursued his plan of reviving the Roman Empire in all its glory and power. He made a name for himself not only as a power politician of the first degree but also as a patron of the arts (the "Carolingian Renaissance"), particularly as the initiator of a comprehensive educational reform. In the "Admonitio generalis" of 789 he decreed that every monastery should have a school and school books.

If we look at older history books on the Holy Roman Empire in the High Middle Ages, the German Empire usually appears to have been an uninterrupted series of individual rulers and dynasties which, if they did what the law and the Church told them to do, exercised almost unrestricted power. According to traditional books, it was not so much social forces and the general development of events arising from long-term legal, social or economic processes that decided the course of history as prominent personalities. Victorious battles, glorious expeditions to Italy, royal audiences at court and displays of pomp – these formed the outer shell of a German monarchy and Roman Empire whose claim to power recognized only the papacy, which was the second universal authority in western Christianity, as being of equal standing. True, other European kingdoms were becoming increasingly self-confident and had already started criticising this attitude in the 12th century. This criticism gradually turned into resistance and deliberate contempt, but even so, in 1184, Frederick Barbarossa was able to stage a magnificent court convention, a veritable apotheosis of chivalry, in Mainz, attended by about 20,000 knights and important dignitaries from almost all European countries. Four years later he was able to hold another such meeting, again in Mainz, which served as part of the preparations for the third crusade and which, in accordance with his pious goals, he even declared to be a "court convention of Jesus Christ" and "court convention of God." The Christian humility expressed in these terms was an indispensable virtue for the kings and emperors called to the throne and one which the people of the day felt had to be put on public display. On the other hand, it was another aspect of the way Frederick Barbarossa saw himself as ruler. The force and power of this concept are impressive even today and were – at least theoretically, as in Mainz – second only to the demands made by God. The glorious self-presentation of the German monarchy, including the splendour of regular coronations, caused 19th century historians, focussing as they did on leading figures, to write lengthy euphoric descriptions of imperial glory.

Since then, however, we have learnt that historical reality, as is often the case, was a little different. The Holy Roman Emperor, who was, after all, also the king of the German Empire, had not only to come to terms with the papacy and other European powers, but at home was faced by a nobility growing in self-confidence and countering the royal claim to power with demands of its own. These demands were based on laws that are not easy to understand, but which it is essential to know about to comprehend the structures of power within the Holy Roman Empire of the Middle Ages. Before we start examining the relations between the nobility and the monarchy we should, therefore, first turn to the simplest foundations of the political system in mediaeval Germany. These had their origin in the Germanic heritage. The Germanic peoples emerging into the light of history when they swept through Europe in a great wave of migration known as the "Völkerwanderung," were organized in tribes (Goths, Lombards, Alemanni, Franks, Saxons, Frisians, Thuringians, Bavarians, Hessians), to which the individual clans and families belonged. The tribe as such, the *gens*, of the migrations had, however, by absorbing scattered groups, lost its original ethnic unity and should therefore be seen as a cultic unity, a political unity, a legal unity and, above all, a unity based on a common ethnic origin. The tribe as a cultic unity would meet round a central altar, where the performance of cultic rituals created a feeling of belonging together. The concept of a political and legal unity was created by a higher law, the *lex*. This *lex* was only valid for tribe members, namely for the people within the tribe and not for its territory – thus non-members were automatically outside the jurisdiction of this law. At the same time, group feeling was particularly fostered by an ethnic awareness based on the idea that all the members of the tribe were descended from the gods themselves – an idea that was, of course, also tied to cultic customs. This way of thinking saw the tribe as an entity of common descent and established a general kinship for all its members, rather along the lines of a clan. Against this background, it can hardly be necessary to stress not only the importance of cult practices, but also the importance of the people actually carrying out religious acts. The cult served to forge links with the divine ancestors and guaranteed the salvation and well-being of the tribe. The priest or magician performing cultic rites had a prominent political position within the community. Thus was created the *divine king* who, because of his ability to ensure its well-being, was the tribe's leader in times of peace and from whose clan the tribal nobility were often recruited. The function of the divine king was passed on within this clan by inheritance. Of decisive importance was the concept that the lineage of the blood flowing through the veins went directly back to the god regarded as being the origin of the tribe – that it was this lineage that really brought well-being and salvation and that the ability to bring such benefits to the tribe ("*Geblütsheiligkeit*"[1]) was passed on in its purest form from father to son. On the other hand, this ability, which normally only ended with death, was not limited to one single person, but was a feature of the whole clan or family, so that all its members had a latent beneficial effect on the tribe. It is important that on the level of the divine monarchy the idea of inheritance could be extremely deep-rooted.

The divine king was not the only outstanding bearer of a function within the Germanic tribe. At times of great need and distress, especially when there was war, the tribal assembly elected a leader whose energy and suitability, whose *idoneity*, seemed to predestine him to guide the tribe through the forthcoming state of emergency. This was the *duke*, the leader of the armed troops, who was elected for a short time to be in charge of certain ventures, whose followers were absolutely loyal to him and who had to resign when the mission was successfully completed. If, however, he was unsuccessful, he was removed from office and replaced by someone more capable. The concept of election and the idea of idoneity were united in the person of the Germanic duke. This was the origin of electoral law, which primarily heeded qualities of leadership and attached less importance to the ability to bring well-being and salvation.

The migrations of the tribes through Europe caused profound changes. Waves of advancing migrants fought the previous settlers and drove them on to unknown regions. The accelerating pace of the advance made the intervals of peace shorter and the periods of war longer. In these changed circumstances, the position of the duke increased whilst

Franconian helmet of state (c. 600)
The Germanic tribes recognized two main sovereign rulers – the sacral, or divine, king, who led the tribe in times of peace, and the military king (duke), who was in charge during periods of war. Tribal migrations led to the two positions being merged into one; from then on, the military leader embodied sovereign authority and the well-being of the tribe. After the tribes had settled down, the duke became the king of the tribe.

the authority of the divine king, whose very existence was only justified by his ability to bring fortune and well-being to the tribe, grew weaker. As the migrating tribes, exposed as they were to the permanent threat of danger, continued their march through Europe for decades, developments were such that the duke retained his function indefinitely until, finally, he took over that of the divine king, i. e. the duke and the divine king became one and the same person – the *martial king*[2], who now embodied the ability to rule and the well-being of the tribe. After the tribe had settled in one place, the martial king became the king of the tribe. When this happened the concepts of inheritance and electoral law, the right of lineage and idoneity all merged to form one unity without, however, losing any of their typical features and becoming inseparable in the process. It was here that the seed was sown for the basic conflict between the laws of succession and electoral laws – a conflict that played such an important role in the German Middle Ages and which took on particularly virulent forms in the election of the king.

Once the tribes had ceased their migrations and the land of the Franks was being conquered, the Merovingian dynasty (who had, mainly by force, managed to eliminate all the minor kings competing for power) succeeded in taking over the leadership. The Merovingians, who were to rule the land of the Franks for several centuries, traced their origin directly back to the Germanic demigod Merowech. They embodied *"Geblütsheiligkeit,"* the ability to bring fortune and well-being, the external sign of which was characteristically demonstrated by long hair. They also ruled in the form of a joint monarchy, since all the sons were bearers of salvation and well-being and thus able to govern. This distribution of power meant that the country was repeatedly divided up and there were seemingly endless struggles for the throne. In the final analysis, the Merovingian dynasty was so weakened by this that their last kings were little more than puppets. This allowed the Carolingian dynasty a rapid rise to power, the basis of which was the office of Mayor of the Palace.

It was by no means easy to remove the Merovingian dynasty from power, as the Carolingians were obviously not able to lay claim to royal salvation, which could only be passed on from father to son. It was Pepin the Younger (751–768) who succeeded in doing so. Mainly by using a firm hand, he had in effect risen to become the sole ruler in the Frankish Empire. Pepin had supported the reforms of Frankish church organisation started by Boniface, thus further deepening the close relations between the pope in Rome and the Carolingian palace mayors. It was thus an obvious step for him to look there for support for his plans for a change of government. A delegation sent to Pope Zacharias in 749 to ask the decisive question whether he could approve of the kings in the Frankish Empire at that time not having royal power *(regalis potestas)* was given the desired answer that "it is better to call him king who has power than he who has remained without royal authority." The report in the Annals of the Frankish Empire adds that the pope, by virtue of his apostolic authority, had ordered Pepin to be made king so that the order of the world *(ordo)* would not be disturbed. Strengthened by this legitimation by the Church of his claim to power, Pepin had himself elected king and, at the same time, anointed by a bishop. The last nominal Merovingian king was given a monk's tonsure and sent to a monastery for the rest of his life, i. e. he lost his long hair, the sign of his royal ability to benefit the people, and with it – irrevocably – his right to be king. Thus ended the Merovingian dynasty and the Carolingian dynasty took over.

The court chapel in Aachen with Charlemagne's throne
When Otto the Great was elected king in 936, his coronation took place in Aachen – a conscious return to an imperial tradition of the Franks. He adorned himself with the Frankish coronation regalia, had himself anointed by the archbishops of Mainz and Trier and finally sat on Charlemagne's throne. In this way, he symbolically joined the ranks of Frankish rulers.

The Feudal System (from the "Heidelberger Sachsenspiegel," c. 1330)
The feudal system was organised according to the medieval ordo. The king enfeoffed spiritual and temporal princes with a sceptre or flag benefice (picture 1). Within a year and a day, the king had to pass on a flag benefice to imperial princes (picture 2); imperial princes, in their turn, could give fiefs to subjects, known as vassals, although these generally had to be of noble descent (picture 4 – a peasant, a merchant and a woman are being refused a fief). Only in exceptional cases could non-noblemen be enfeoffed (picture 5), and they could not bequeath their benefices.

It is probable that there were similar things happening in the Frankish Empire between A. D. 749 and A. D. 751 as there were within the tribes during the period of the migrations across Europe, when the divine kings disappeared and the martial kings established themselves as bifunctional bearers of power and well-being. There can be no doubt that, constitutionally, election by the tribe was the true constitutive act and the election element therefore the basis for future claims to the title of king. But election alone was not sufficient. True, he who had the idoneity was called to the throne, but this did not include the ability to bring fortune to the people. Here was a problem that still needed solving. The Church stepped into this gap by helping the king to the necessary sacral consecration by anointing him. Thus, the Germanic concept of fortune and salvation through divine lineage was replaced by consecration by the Church – an act that was sacramental in character. When Pope Stephen II came to the Frankish Empire in 753, he both reanointed the King and anointed Pepin's two sons, i. e. the king's potential successors. This meant the monarchy was no longer bound to traditional concepts and had set off along the path to the divine right of kings. Ties between the royal dynasty, the *stirps regia,* and the Church took on a new dimension, both because the ideological foundations of power were now being increasingly more firmly tied to the Christian concept of the world, and because consecration by the Church, in contrast to the process of election, was the element of continuity that excluded the aspirations of others. Looked at from this point of view, Charlemagne's intensive efforts to convert the people to Christianity – efforts which increasingly repressed the Germanic concept of the sanctity of kings – could be interpreted as being a strategy to retain and consolidate power. By the middle of the 8th century only a relatively small section of the population had become "Christian" in the true sense of the word and an increase was needed.

When the Merovingian dynasty disappeared from the scene, the supporting parts of the basis of royal rule finally disintegrated. The *trustis regia,* the king's closest followers, must first be mentioned, who, in accordance with the Germanic concept of allegiance, were bound to the ruler by a voluntary bond of loyalty. The ruler had given them protection and in return they performed war service for him. After the change of power the *antrustions,* the members of the *trustis regia,* belonged just as much to a past age as did the office of mayor of the palace, which from then on the Merovingians left vacant so that other dynasties would not be able to use it to seize power. It was, however, imperative for the retention of power for every nobleman (until the Merovingians forbade it) in a position to give protection to have a reliable circle of followers loyal to the king. The decline of the *trustis regia* left a gap, which during the Carolingian period was filled with a newly formed constitutional instrument that was to become one of the mainstays of the state in the German Empire of the Middle Ages – the feudal system.

The foundation of the feudal system consisted of three intertwined elements. To begin with, we must take a look at vassalage. This was a condition already known in the latter stages of the classical world and based on Roman civil law. The term comes from "gwas," the Celtic word for "squire" which became "vassus, vasallus" in Latin. It denotes a man who, for reasons of economic need, entered into a condition of dependence, had to serve a master for the rest of his life and was duty-bound to obey him; in return for this the master had to guarantee the man's livelihood. The vassal was originally a serf, thus belonging to a lower stratum of society, and had entered the state of dependence by means of an act of submission, the *commendation*. Central to this act was a ceremony that involved the master enclosing the vassal's folded hands in his – a gesture both of submission and protection.

The second aspect to be mentioned was the tangible element, the *beneficium, feudum,* feudal benefice or fief. The forerunner of the fief was the *precarium* in the late antique world – property transferred to the recipient in return for the payment of a due for his own use or beneficial interest. Under the Carolingians – and this development started at the latest under Karl Martell, who was mayor of the palace between 714 and 741 – feudal land, which often used to belong to the Church, was transferred to vassals, who now had to do military service as a substitute for the retinue the nobility had been forbidden to keep. However, carrying weapons was the same thing as the ability to provide protec-

Emperor Otto the Great (equestrian statue, Magdeburg, c. 1240)
When Henry I of Saxony succeeded the Franconians to the throne in 919, he was crowned by the dukes as "primus inter pares." His son Otto I, the Great, on the other hand, was already designated by his father to succeed him in 929 and crowned in 936. One of the most important things he did during his reign of almost 40 years (936–973) was to missionize the Slavs after his victory over the Hungarians in 955.

tion, and this was really a privilege of free citizens. This development led to the social position of the vassals being raised, so that in the course of time it became an attractive proposition for free citizens to become vassals. The Carolingians saw this as a way of creating a circle of followers entirely dependent upon them.

It was significant that in addition to the two elements mentioned above there was a third, one that was inseparable from them, namely fealty, i. e. the obligation of fidelity on the part of the vassal to his lord. This is not a moral notion. Rather, it originated in the idea behind the concept of retainers and denoted a bond based on an oath of allegiance between the free follower and his master – a bond that was binding for both of them without, however, encroaching on the freedom of the follower. After the decline of the old retaining system, the element of fealty was, as it were, available again and became part of the feudal system, which now – and only now – assumed its final form. Feudal service and fealty were united. Logically, the vassal could now only be a free man or a member of the nobility. But now he had to take an oath of fealty at the same time as the commendation and, during the investiture, was usually granted a fief, for which he was required to render certain necessary services. These services were taken to be *consilium et auxilium*, i. e. counsel and aid. Aid, of course, essentially meant military assistance, i. e. an obligation to perform military service by providing a contingent of soldiers. Counsel was not least taken to mean sitting on the jury in court when judgement was to be passed on cases involving feudal law, such as felony and breaches of the oath of fealty. The feudal lord in his turn granted not only the benefice but also gave protection, so that we can assume that the agreement was binding to both parties. By granting benefices, the feudal system allowed all members of the nobility to set up their own body of retainers. This consisted of vassals and lesser vassals. But at the top of this ladder there was always the king – the leader, the supreme feudal lord and in the final analysis the central nub of all legal ties connected with feudalism. This is the feudal pyramid and it incorporated the nobility within it, so that any pretensions to rule based on possession of allodium were, at the outset, given constitutional restrictions. This system was rounded off by the fact that offices and positions held *(honores)* were also included. Not only were the noble office-bearers granted feudal benefices in return for the tasks they were commissioned by the king to perform, but the offices themselves were made into feudal benefices or treated as such and, via the norms of feudal law, bound to the king.

On the one hand, this feudalization of the structure of the state, a state based on institutions, drew the nobility into a linkage of the exercise of power and the delegation of government – a linkage which guaranteed the prominent position of the monarchy, independent of the recognition of its divine roots; on the other hand, it subjected the rulers themselves to the norms of feudal law, including refusal to do military service in certain cases, and exposed them to all the dangers and risks a possible disintegration of these institutions would involve. Such risks would, for example, be double or multiple vassalage, i. e. commitments to one or more overlords or the inheritability of the feudal benefice, both of which were developments that were made explosive by the weakness of the Carolingian monarchy in the 9th century. If we talk of the centrifugal power of the feudal system that took effect during the decline of the Carolingian age, we not only mean the invalidation of the principle

The Marksburg near Braubach on the Rhine (building begun at the beginning of the 13th century)
In the Middle Ages, the possession of castles was inseparable from the lifestyle of the nobility and, in the 12th century, led to the feudalization process. The first ruler to pursue a policy of large-scale castle building was Henry IV (d. 1106) in an attempt to consolidate his sovereignty. This development peaked in the building of fortresses by the Staufer, particularly the imperial palatinates of Frederick Barbarossa, which were to be found all over the entire Empire and not only had a military function, but also clearly a symbolic one – they were used by the Staufer to document their claim to power.

of Charlemagne (768–814) and Louis the Pious (814–840) that a vassal could only serve one master if he was to be in a position to abide by his oath of allegiance. We also mean that if a vassal died, the laws of inheritance came into play, as it were, giving the heir a natural claim to succeed both to the office and the benefice.

The Capitulary of Quierzy (877), in which Charles the Bald (840–877) made arrangements on this point, was an important landmark as far as this was concerned, although he refused to allow his regulations to be valid over and beyond the present situation. As it was, the decline of the Carolingians led to the unrestrained continuation of the aforesaid regulations, and these eventually became customary and hence legally binding. In the long term, the inefficiency of the central power of the monarchy (which had political causes and which could no longer stop the forces within the constitution of the empire from drifting apart) led to the idea of inheritance being incorporated into feudal law. But if the laws of inheritance could be used to pass on one individual nobleman's official authority and his benefice, then according to feudal law this must also hold good for the leader, i. e. the king. Thus consecration, the laws of inheritance and feudal laws were all on the same plane. Initially, however, this had no effect since the Carolingian dynasty died out, to be followed by the Saxon dynasty.

If we investigate the independent foundations of power of the nobility in the Middle Ages, it becomes clear that these were not to be found in the possession of a benefice, since such a benefice – no matter whether it was an office or land – was originally "lent out" and could be withdrawn if the vassal neglected the duties connected with it. Every nobleman had to prove the existence of allodial possessions, independent of a benefice, which – as they were his own – he could bequeath, sell, give away and exchange as he wished. If it were to be profitably run, this personal property (and usually of course the beneficial, the feudal estate, as well) was organized as a manorial estate. At the heart of this system, which is usually defined as seigniory over both the land and the people, was the feudal manor. The feudal manor and the surrounding lands, the *demesne*, were run by the lord of the manor himself with the help of domestic labour. Clustered around this area were the peasants' tenements and, on larger estates, farms held on lease, in which there would live the *serfs* and *cottagers*, i. e. bonded peasants, who made up the greatest part of the extended family serving the feudal lord and bound to render praedial services. The lord provided protection and patronage both for the inner region of the feudal manor and the families living there and for the entire complex of the manorial estate. He also exercised simple legal rights which are thought to originate in the old German *domiciliary right*, i. e. right of authority within one's own house. This right meant nothing more than that the head of the house gave protection to all the people belonging to the immediate sphere of his house, be they members of the family, be they servants and labourers. The protection he gave them entitled him to pass judgement over any crimes they might commit. The established right to give protection and pass judgement was the origin of seigniorial rights. These did not have to be specially granted by the state and are generally called the autonomous laws of nobility. They were gradually joined by the permanent exercise of functions of power, such as the authority exercised by counts[3], which was originally assigned by the monarchy and then taken away and incorporated into the assets of individual families of nobility

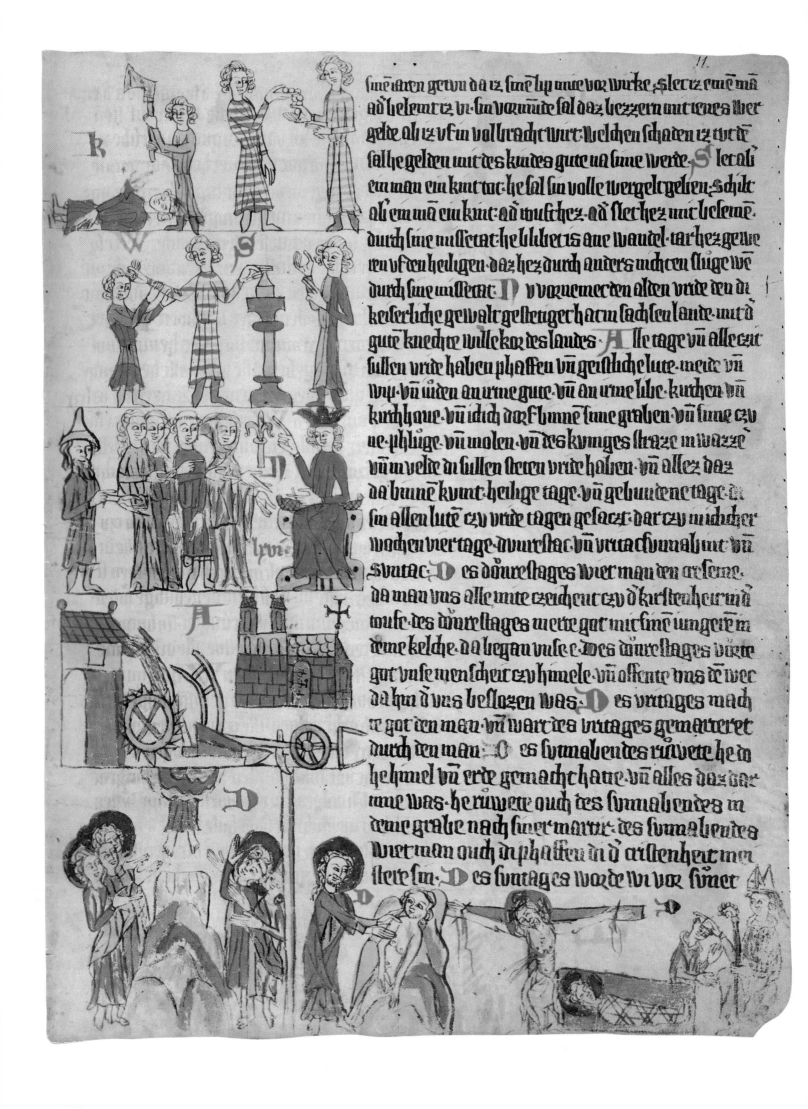

sine iaren getun da iz sine lip ane vor wirke. slet iz eine man
ad belemet iz. vn sin vormunde sal daz bezzern mit ienes wer
gelde als iz vf in vollbracht wirt. Welchen schaden iz tut der
sal he gelden mit des kindes gute na sime werde. Slet al
ein man ein kint tot. he sal sin volle wergelt gelen. Schit
als ein man ein kint. ad wuschez. ad stechez mit beseme.
durch sine missetat. he blibet iz ane wandel. tar hez gewe
ren vf den heiligen. daz hez durch anders nichten sluge we
durch sine missetat. Dv vorneme den alden vride den du
keiserliche gewalt gesetzet hat in sachsen lande. unt de
gute knechte willekor des landes. Alle tage vn allezit
sullen vride haben phaffen vn geistliche lute. meide vn
wip. vn iuden an irme gute. vn an irme libe. kirchen vn
kirchhove. vn iclich dorf binne sine graben. vn sine zu
ve phlige. vn molen. vn des kuninges straze in wazze
vn in velde di sullen steten vride haben. vn allez daz
da binne kunt. heilige tage. vn gebundene tage. di
sin allen lute zu vride tagen gesatzt. dar zu iclicher
wochen vier tage. donrestag. vn vritach. sunnabent. vn
suntac. Des donrestages wirt man den aresme
da man uns alle mite zeichent zu de kirsteheit. in
toufe. des donrestages wette got mit sime iungeren in
sime kelche. da begap unse e. des donrestages virte
got unse menscheit zu himele. vn offente uns de wec
da hin de uns beslozen was. Des vritages mach
te got den man. vn wart des vritages gemarteret
durch den man. Des sunnabendes rivete he do
he himel vn erde gemacht hatte. vn alles daz dar
inne was. he rivete ouch des sunnabendes in
deme grabe nach siner martir. des sunnabendes
wirt man ouch di phaffen in de cristenheit mit
stere sin. Des suntages worde wi vor siner

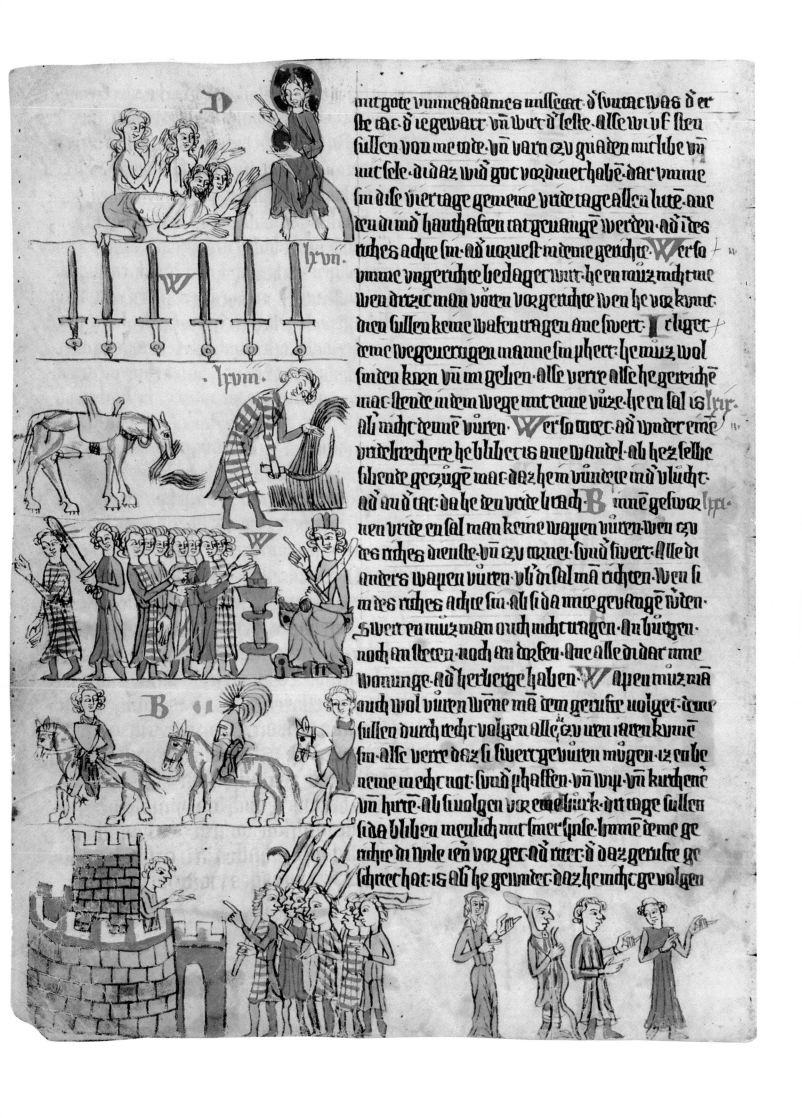

mit gote vnne adames nissent d suntac was d er
ste tac d ie gewart vn wart d leste. Alle wurf sten
sullen von me voe. vn varn czu gnaden mit libe vn
mit sele. al daz wil got vordinet habe. dar vmme
sin dise viertage gemeine vride tage allen lute. ane
den di vm hauthaften tat geuange werden. ad ines
riches achte sin. ad vorquest in deme gerichte. Wer so
vmme vngerichte bedaget wirt. he en muz nicht me
wen dirzic man vuren vor gerichte. wen he vor kumt
den sullen keine wafen tragen ane swert. I cliget
deme wege vertagen manne sin pherr. he muz wol
siden korn vn im geien. alle verre alse he gereichen
mac. stende in dem wege mit eine vuze. he en sal is
nicht deme vuren. Wer so wiret ad under eine
vorbrechere he blibet is ane mantel. ab hez selbe
siteute gezuge mac. daz hem vundere in d vlucht
ad an d tat. da he den vride brach. B inne geswor
nen vride en sal man keine wapen vuren. wen czu
des riches dienste. vn czu turnei. sunder swert. Alle di
anders wapen vuren. vn in sal man richten. Wen si
in des riches achte sin. ab si da inne geuange wden.
swert en muz man ouch nicht tragen. An burgen
noch an steten. noch an dorsen. ane alle di dar inne
wonunge. ad herberge haben. W apen muz man
ouch wol vuren. wene man dem geruste volget. dem
sullen durch recht volgen alle. czu wen iaren kumen
sin. alse verre daz si swert geuuren mugen. iz en be
neme iecht not. sunder phassen. vn wip. vn kuchene
vn hirte. ab si volgen vor eine burc. in tage sullen
si da bliben nienlich mit siner spise. inme me ge
richte di inne sin. vor gen. ad wer d daz geruste ge
schret hat. is ab he geruiret. daz he nicht ge volgen

Dú Lantgre
vin võ dúringe.

Lantgrãne hmã
von dúringen.

hie kriegret mit lange h walth võ d vogilweide. h wolfrã von eschilbach
h reimander alte. der tugenthafte schriber henrich võ ofteringe
vñ klingeſor von vngerlant.

The provinces of the Empire paying homage to Otto III (detail, c. 1000)
Like his predecessors before him (Otto the Great and Otto II), Otto III (983–1002) tried to use the Church as one of the pillars of sovereign rule. His plan was to return to Rome its old position as the centre of the globe and renew the Roman Empire. Otto's veneration of Charlemagne shows that in the final instance he wanted to revive the Carolingian view of the emperor. His untimely death, however, prevented him from putting his far-reaching ideas into practice. The miniature shows the youthful ruler in coronation regalia, with spiritual and temporal rulers at either side of the throne.

54

as hereditary functionary fief. It was this level of law and sovereignty, based as it was on personal assets and inaccessible to the monarchy and its officials, that made it possible for the nobility to build up a political position of its own. The nobility saw itself as an association freely formed to put mutual ideas into practice. The members of an association were always of equal standing, and the only way the spokesman or leader, the *primus inter pares,* could ever be chosen was by election. This attitude of the nobility, which had its roots in old Germanic ideas, with their emphasis on the principle of election to office, was to turn out to be one of the biggest obstacles to the monarchy's plans for succession.

As the Carolingian Empire gradually dissolved and the Holy Roman Empire started taking shape, a nobility came onto the scene endowed with a growing self-confidence. Instead of the nobility in the Carolingian Empire, whose only interests were the monarchy and the consolidation of their own prominent position, we now have associations of nobility who made sure of their right of representation within the subregions of the Empire and who were able to get the king to accept their point of view. The first signs of this process can already be found in the amendment to the Treaty of Verdun at the negotiations in Coulaines (843) for the West Frankish Empire, the effects of which were also clearly to be seen in the East Frankish Empire with the fall of Charles the Fat (876–888) in 887. It finally led to a few noble families amassing property and rights. This, in turn, was the origin of the rule of the nobility in the tribes known to 19th century historians as the "Younger Tribal Duchies." In 919, Henry I (919–936), the Duke of Saxony, was the first German king to be elected who was not a Frank, who was not designated by blood ties and who consciously adopted sovereign rule as *primus inter pares.* Anointment had previously served the legal continuation of the lineage. But Henry circumspectly refused to be anointed, which was typical of this idea that a king should rule on the strength of election to office. According to ancient custom, the tribe of the Franks appeared on the scene as the leading tribe in the empire, the "imperial people." The Saxons joined forces with them in unanimous support of the principle of election.

Things were already different when Henry's son, Otto the Great (936–973), came to the throne. An internal "house order" prematurely chose Otto as the sole successor to the throne in 929, thus cancelling the principle of partition. Early in 936 he was officially designated by his father to succeed him. His accession to the throne with his election and coronation in Aachen on 7th August, 936, again harked back to the traditions of the Frankish Empire, and he showed this to the world by wearing the dress of the Franks. At the centre of the ceremony were the presentation of the insignia, anointment and coronation by the archbishops of Mainz and Cologne, followed by him sitting on the throne, Charlemagne's marble throne, a second time. The four dukes – the Duke of Lorraine as the chamberlain, the Duke of Franconia as the lord high steward, the Duke of Swabia as the cup-bearer and the Duke of Bavaria as the marshal – symbolically performed the ceremonial services during the coronation feast at the end of the ceremony. Accession to the throne and homage rendered by important personages from the secular world, preceded by a "pre-election" by the Franconian and Saxon "imperial people," the events in Aachen – all these were merely the worldly, the formal part of the ceremony. The coronation banquet, on the other hand, made it clear that the emphasis of the power exercised by the

ILL. PAGE 52:
Frederick Barbarossa and his sons (c. 1200)
Few German Emperors in the high Middle Ages are still a source of such fascination today as Frederick Barbarossa (1152–1190). His epoch stands out gloriously from the reign of his hapless predecessor, Conrad III. His personality reflects the power and the glory of the united empire, which after his death slowly began to disintegrate under the burden of internal power struggles. The picture shows Frederick seated on the throne in the middle, with his sons, Henry VI and Frederick, Duke of Swabia, on either side.

ILL. PAGE 53:
The Landgrave and Landgravine of Thuringia
(Große Heidelberger Liederhandschrift, beginning of the 14th century)
The emperors of the Holy Roman Empire repeatedly had to defend their sovereignty against the often bitter resistance of spiritual and temporal princes. When Henry VI did all he could in 1196 to introduce hereditary monarchy, he met with great opposition from the princes. The leader of his antagonists was the Landgrave of Thuringia pictured here.

Gregory the Great (540–604; from the Olmütz Horologium, c. 1140)
By descent Gregory the Great was a Roman nobleman. In 590 he was elected to St. Peter's chair and is thus regarded as being the first of the medieval popes. Before his pontificate, Gregory was a Benedictine monk, abbot and founder of several monasteries. By resolutely following his monastic ideals, he consolidated the position of the pope in the face of temporal political influences. It is due to his influence, for example, that the positions in the papal household were occupied exclusively by clerics. The description "first medieval pope" would seem to be justified in view of the fact that Gregory's strictly clerical policies must be seen in the context of subsequent disputes between pope and emperors in the Investiture Contest.

dukes was to be on its official character. The power of the dukes was thus restricted in a vital way and, in the final analysis, related to the monarchy.

In view of these premises, we can hardly be surprised at the many rebellions among the nobility that shook the governments of Otto I and his son Otto II (961–983). Neither can we be surprised at the resurgence in the Emperor's power and attempts to use the Imperial Church as one of the mainstays of sovereign rule. A return to the practices of Louis the Pious, who had put the bishoprics and monasteries beyond the influence of the nobility by giving them immunity and the protection of the monarchy, thus making them into churches with advowsons held by the king, i. e. bases of power for the monarchy, very much corresponded to the need for the growing sacralization of the monarch's position. The Empire and the Church, with their diverging forces, were held together by the holiness of the monarchy.

Without wanting to go into the details of these developments here, I must nevertheless emphasize that the king's sacral, even sacerdotal position within the Church was vital for the engagement of the Imperial

Church in the stabilization of the power of the monarchy against the nobility. It was this particular role that raised the king above the masses and justified his influence on important Church matters such as appointments in the bishoprics. It was this particular role that guaranteed ecclesiastical and secular authorities working together in the interests of maintaining the power of the monarchy. The monarchy of the Ottonians and Salians, influenced as it was by imperial ideology, even claimed the right to control the papacy.

Bearing this in mind, it becomes clear what far-reaching consequences the reform movement within the Church in the 11th century had for the position of the German monarchy and for the structures of power in the Empire. The *libertas ecclesiae,* the liberty of the Church, not only meant fighting such obvious wrongs as the buying and selling of spiritual offices and priests marrying, but first and foremost the elimination of lay influences within the official Church hierarchy. But the king, too, was regarded as belonging to the laity – a point of view that took account of a new understanding of the sacerdotal function and which the Church was able to assert in the ensuing Investiture Contest. On the face of it, this controversy was about the right to appoint bishops – who generally belonged to the nobility – by exhausting the possibilities offered by feudal law. In reality, however, it was about the use of the Imperial Church as an instrument of power. The conflict was settled with a compromise laid down in the Concordat of Worms in 1122. The king agreed to renounce the traditional investiture of the newly elected prelate with ring and staff and permitted free canonical elections and consecration, and in return the pope conceded both the right of the king to be present at elections of bishops and abbots and a limited degree of influence on controversial decisions. The regalia and the property, rights and income due to the monarchy were conferred by the king with the sceptre before consecration. For this, the newly elected prelate had to swear homage and fealty to the king. From then on, the spiritual princes were bound to the monarchy by ties of feudal law without there being a danger of them indulging in multiple vassalage and bequeathing their benefices. This meant that feudal law – which since the end of the Carolingian epoch had, as a ruling instrument, become ambivalent for the power of the monarchy – was given a clearly definable constitutional function. This function was initially limited to the relationship between the king and Church, but could apparently be extended at any time. The conscious feudalization of the constitution of the Imperial Church by the Concordat of Worms opened the door to the concept of the Holy Roman Empire as an imperial feudal system headed by the king.

In the meantime, the nobility living in the Empire had also undergone a complex development and during the 11th century was even in the throws of nothing less than a constitutional upheaval. At one time, individual aristocratic families had seen their descent more from a biological and genealogical point of view without, however, a feeling for the family as a group that encompasses many generations. About now, however, families started seeing themselves as a historically and socially continuous lineage – one which had its roots in the memorable deeds of some great ancestor. The noble family created a focal point for all its branches. This was usually a castle with a monastery containing the family grave. The members of the family started calling themselves after this castle, which, roughly speaking, was in the centre of the property and embodied their privileges. Genealogies came into being, mostly in

Henry IV kneeling before Matilda of Tuscany
(from the "Vita Mathildis," 1114)
Since it was impossible to avoid appointing clerics to administer the Empire, kings and emperors, i. e. members of the laity, claimed the right to appoint high spiritual dignitaries. This was a practice that led to great disagreement between emperors and popes; but it did not escalate until the quarrel between Henry IV und Gregory VII (1073–1085). When Henry called for Gregory to abdicate in 1076, the Pope excommunicated Henry. Henry had little choice but to apologize. In 1077, Henry set off on his difficult journey to Canossa, which ended with the reconciliation of the two adversaries. The picture shows Henry kneeling before Matilda of Tuscany and Hugo, Abbot of Cluny, whom he had asked to intercede on his behalf with the pope.

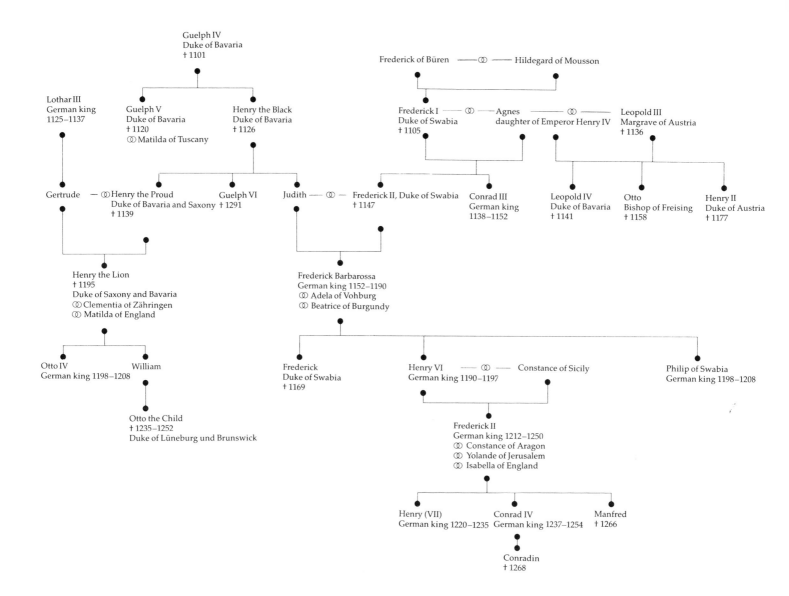

Genealogy of the Staufer and Guelphs

For about 130 years after Conrad III, the Hohenstaufen dynasty dominated events in the German Empire. The Staufer reign was overshadowed by disputes with the Guelphs, whose most colourful representative was Henry the Lion. In spite of this, however, the Staufer rule brought Germany a period of relative security and stability, and this in its turn allowed culture to flourish; literature and architecture, in particular, developed amazingly.

the vicinity of the family's monastery, and told of the family's history since the days of its founder – a history that was as often as not intertwined with mythological elements – and at the same time showed coats of arms which had evolved as a sign of identification during the post-1095 crusades. This new conception the nobility had of itself went hand in hand with a changing concept of laws.

For one thing, the *leges*, the old tribal laws which had given the ethnically homogeneous community a legal and political framework, had lost their original function – probably because of the growing Christianization of the nobility and the members of the tribe – and had disappeared during the 10th century. It is not clear exactly how this happened, but at the end of the process there remained only the nobility, which was now legally a confederation and through which a new kind of law came into being – territorial law. Keeping the peace and the lowest level of jurisdiction, autonomous laws of the nobility that arose from individual rights as master of the house in manor and castle – these were the manorial foundation for claims by the Association of the German nobility, organized in the provincial diet of the nobility, to have a say in decisions directly affecting them. The most important decision, however, concerned the question of the succession to the throne. Because like ranks had joined together in one association, their concept of law was very coherent. As far as the succession to the throne was concerned, the nobility saw it as a process that had to take place according to criteria laid down in electoral law. The concept of electoral right – which was finally victorious – grew increasingly deeper roots during the 12th century.

For another thing, remarkable progress had been made during the 11th century as far as jurisdiction was concerned. It was now possible to separate rights and property. In other words, it was no longer necessary to own land to be able to exercise the rights of sovereignty connected with it. Thus, if a government by the nobility was to be set up or extended, it sufficed to reserve the rights of sovereignty or to collect them in one hand, whereas landed property could be passed on with the aim of establishing useful connections. There was also another aspect that came to the fore. Ecclesiastical property, be it a bishop's or a monastery's, was also organized as a manorial estate – and enjoyed immunity, i. e. it was exempt from secular law. Jurisdiction became a problem after the appearance of "blood jurisdiction," i. e. the death penalty, since according to Church law it was forbidden to "drink blood." If it was to administer justice and protect its temporal sovereign rights, the Church was forced to nominate a nobleman as an administrator, who was officially allowed to lift the immunity, hold court and collect taxes. The acquisition of bailiwicks – rights of sovereignty which the noble bailiff and his heirs could keep continuous possession of – was one of the most important aspects in establishing a closely knit government by the nobility. But not even the Crown lands of the Empire were a hindrance when it came to filling gaps by acquiring titles to land. In doing so, it was not necessary to create a completely comprehensive complex of property and rights. A network of islands of property and rights were enough to pave the way for territorial government.

Of all these processes on the level of the constitution, the monarchy was affected most when it was a matter of regulating the succession to the throne in the case of a dynasty dying out on the male side or there being no male successor available who had reached the age of majority.

St. John's chapel in Pürgg castle
From the 11th century on, the nobility's growing self-confidence and their new conception of themselves led them not only to build castles but frequently also to establish monasteries on their own land. As a general rule, the family tomb was in these private monasteries, and the clerics living here would pray for the salvation of the souls of the dead. However, these monasteries served not only pious aims – it was here that chronicles were written and genealogical tables recorded in honour and praise of the noble family; it was here, too, that plans were made to open up new land.

Conrad III (Miniature from the "Kölner Königschronik," about 1240)
Conrad III, who reigned 1138–1152, was the uncle of Frederick Barbarossa. His rule was a period of misfortune – Conrad not only had to ward off the claims of powerful imperial princes, especially the Guelphs, but also had to bear the burden of the failure of the Second Crusade (1147–49). The reason for the defeat in the Holy Land was that there was no cooperation between the French and the German armies.

The more the regional nobility was influenced by provincial law, the greater was its tendency to insist on electoral law being observed. Provincial law did not have equally strong roots in all areas. As a result, the elections of the 12th century kings – after the transition from tribal electoral law to the electoral law of important noblemen had been completed – became a complicated struggle between the various groups of nobility. It is tempting to talk of differences between the north and south of the country, but this would be an over-simplification. In the northern areas of the Empire, particularly on the Lower Rhine, in Westphalia and in Saxony, the nobility was mainly geared to common law and therefore favoured election according to electoral law. The nobility in the southern and southwestern parts of the Empire, where the centre of the Crown lands was and where ties according to feudal law were all the more intensive, favoured laws of inheritance and the existence of blood ties as a solution to the question of succession to the throne. Certainly, care was generally taken that the chosen candidate was in some way related to the previous dynasty – and this was hardly difficult in view of the close family ties within the upper stratum of the nobility – but even so, the fact that the idea of election had increasingly been gaining ground by the 13th century cannot be overlooked. New royal dynasties came into being as a result of the elections in 1024 (when the Salian Conrad II, 1024–1039, took over from the Saxon dynasty), 1077 (when the Swabian Duke Rudolf of Rheinfelden, 1077–1080, was chosen to be king against the Salian Henry IV, 1056–1106), 1081 (when Count Hermann of Salm, 1081–1088, was elected to succeed Rudolf), 1125 (when Duke Lothar of Saxony, 1125–1137, succeeded the last Salian, Henry V, 1106–1125), and 1138 (when Conrad III of Staufen, 1138–1152, came to the throne by means of a *coup d'état*). The events of 1077 can be seen as the first free elections of a German king, and in 1138 the principle of free elections had asserted itself as a legally recognized basis for the succession to the throne.

The result of this was that any powerful prince of high birth could become king. Frederick Barbarossa (1152–1190) was already to discover this in 1152, when he set out to succeed his uncle Conrad III. It was only with great difficulty and by means of skilful negotiations and promises that he managed to persuade the Frankfurt election meeting to accept such a solution without the purely electoral character of the events being called in question. Irrespective of the question of whether the Guelph Henry the Lion, Duke of Saxony and finally – probably as the result of concessions made in Frankfurt – also Duke of Bavaria, was a rival candidate in the election of the king in 1152, he was a powerful imperial prince and in any case a potential successor to the throne. His marriage to the daughter of Henry II of England also put him above his equals. It is not for nothing that he is said to have wanted to become king. The fact was clearly expressed in a miniature in the Helmarshausen Gospels, where we can see Henry the Lion and his wife Matilda, the Duke and Duchess, being crowned with royal crowns by Christ himself in the presence of their ancestors, including two kings (Lothar III and Henry II of England)[4]. By claiming royalty, Henry's aim was to give his principality, indeed his coming sovereignty, a final constitutional frame. Basically, this only reflected, on a higher level, the efforts of other princes to consolidate their own territorial rule and make it impervious to outside interference. The Staufer monarchy was largely powerless in the face of such developments, since it had no way of legally interfering at a provincial level. In view of this situation, the royal court and royal chancellery

The coronation of Henry the Lion and his wife, Matilda (Gospel Book of Henry the Lion, c. 1188) Henry the Lion, Duke of Saxony and Bavaria, opposed the Staufer Frederick Barbarossa in his election in 1152. He was one of the most powerful of the imperial princes and posed a continual threat to the rule of the Staufer until he was deposed (between 1178 and 1180). The miniature clearly shows that he was a potential heir to the throne and cherished the hope of becoming king – Henry the Lion and his wife Matilda, herself the daughter of a king, are being crowned in the presence of their ancestors.

took to viewing the structure of the Empire from a standpoint that was legally strictly feudal and ignoring any other legal conceptions. This attitude not only had the advantage that the position of the king at the very top of the pyramid was indisputable, that he had full authority and all others in power were subordinate to him. It also allowed the interpretation that succession to the throne was, as was common in feudal law, hereditary. From then on, in a kind of latent dualism, there was to be dissension between the feudal conceptions supported by the monarchy and the leaning of parts of the nobility towards common law. This was particularly true when it came to nominating the monarch, especially as far as the question of election vs. inheritance was concerned.

Since scholastic thinking and ecclesiastical law had in the meantime, however, taught the people to systematize the whole legal set-up, and since also the Italian policies of the Staufer meant that norms of Roman law were regularly being introduced into the Empire, it was a matter of course for the new ruling order to be viewed as universal. The feudal pyramid was really only loosely structured. The *Heerschild* order contained the seven ranks defining the position of vassals within the feudal hierarchy. Below the monarch at the top were the spiritual and

The imperial seal of Frederick Barbarossa (c. 1155) In the Middle Ages, seals were an important part of the legal system. Emperors and kings had always used seals – depicting them seated on thrones and holding the insignia of their power (see picture) – to authenticate documents and decrees. But a seal was not the privilege of princes, for in the 11th century there were already seals belonging to counts – but in contrast to rulers, the nobility were not shown sitting "majestically." In the 12th century, towns and monasteries started using seals to document their legal position.

temporal princes, slightly apart from each other and on places two and three; then came the earls, free lords, *Schöffenbarfreie* and *ministeriales* as vassals and sub-vassals; the seventh and lowest rank was the knight with one shield, who could be granted fief but not pass it on. This structure of the Empire was limited to the nobility, for until then no one else could be enfeoffed. It thus largely ignored political reality, which was increasingly recognizing the importance of the towns and the bourgeoisie. The position of the monarchy at the top of the temporal hierarchy of power was, however, consolidated in this order, which was why the feudal constitution of the German Empire was to remain in force until after the Middle Ages, despite the emergence of territorial rule. But it already contained the seed of decline, for the basis of power of the imperial princes did not consist exclusively of their duchies and countships (which were taken to be imperial fiefs), their fiefs and the rights resulting from these.

The difficulties encountered in completely divesting an imperial prince of the foundations of his rule, if ever his ambitions regarding the monarchy and his aristocratic equals became unbearable, were to become particularly clear when it came to deposing Henry the Lion. In order to remove him from his position of power, it was necessary to start common and feudal law proceedings against him, in the process of which Henry's noble equals took part as judges on a provincial level and tenants-in-chief on an imperial level. Trial and condemnation under feudal law led to Henry being deprived of his feudal estates, i.e. his duchies and all his imperial fiefs. Trial under common law led to him being put under the ban of the Empire and then a double ban, and this included the temporary confiscation of his own lands. His allodial estates were probably reinstated, at least in part, after the removal of the ban and double ban, but his imperial fiefs were lost forever. Henry the Lion's trial, although political in nature, exposed the constitutional roots of the authority of the nobility in common and feudal law. At the same time, the course taken by the trial made it clear that the king was only in a position to deprive an imperial prince of his power on a common law level if he was assisted by the association of nobility – in other words, on this level his claim to power was but limited.

The requirements for acceptance in the rank of an imperial prince were in accordance with this constitutional duality of the foundations of aristocratic rule. For it can be seen that approximately from 1180 onwards (when Henry the Lion's duchies are again made into imperial fiefs by the famous Gelnhausen Charter of 13th April, 1180), and in the course of the alignment of the state by the Staufer to feudal law, the imperial princes closed their ranks downwards, so that special admission had to be granted by the king. This admission, which was, of course, very much in the interests of the direct royal ruling delegation, took place in an act containing a number of steps that must be distinguished from each other: The person pleading admission ceded allodial property to the Empire, which the king then united with the future imperial fief to form a new fief and redistributed as an imperial principality, observing feudal law in the process. In this way, Count Baldwin of Hennegau became the Margrave of Namur (1184/88), Otto the Guelph was made the Duke of Brunswick (1235), and Landgrave Henry of Hesse (1292) and Count Amadeus of Savoy (1310/13) were also raised to their new ranks. Great constitutional significance was attached to the combination of allodium and fief.

It remained to be seen how far the provincial law background of the position of the imperial princes would set limits to the monarchy's demands for unconditional recognition of the feudal and successional structure of the Empire. This became clear in 1196, with the rejection of plans to establish hereditary monarchy in the Empire, and in 1198 with that double election that was to lead to the years-long dispute over the right to the throne. Henry VI (1190–1197) wanted either to have the constitution of the Empire and the law of succession irrevocably linked together or the concept of hereditary monarchy accepted. And each time it was one of the princes from parts of the Empire in which common law concepts were important who put a stop to his plans. In 1196, in an effort to buy concessions, he offered the princes full hereditary rights in their fiefs including the female lineage; to the prelates he offered concession of the right of spoliation[5]. Landgrave Hermann of Thuringia finally came forth as one of the leaders of the resistance to these plans. And in 1198 the Archbishop of Cologne, Adolf of Altena, stood out as one of the most ardent supporters of election rights of the princes and in opposition to the Staufer concept of hereditary succession, to the advantage of Philip of Swabia (1198–1208).

If we bear in mind the persistence of the nobility as a social class, then we can scarcely be surprised that in the late Middle Ages the principle of hereditary succession was finally established, especially as it was also closely connected to the Church. The Golden Bull of 1356 of Charles IV (1346–1378) not only firmly established in the unwritten constitution of the Empire the rights of the electors in the procedure for the election of the king; it also limited the circle of those entitled to vote

Castel del Monte (Apulia, c. 1240)
The Staufer Frederick II (1212-1250) was not only greatly interested in Italy for political reasons; he was also very active in the field of culture – as can be seen, for example, in his founding of Naples University in June 1224. His hunting lodge Castel del Monte, built in 1240, is an impressive illustration of his building activities. The octangular ground plan of the castle is worthy of note.

Timo of Kistritz (founder figure, Naumburg cathedral, c. 1250)
The end of the Staufer rule in Germany (1254) heralded a period of unrest and law-breaking, forcing the nobility to renew imperial authority by a free election of the king during the interregnum (until 1273). As early as 1256, the Frankfurt Diet gave seven electors the absolute right to elect the ruler – three spiritual and four temporal electors demanded capitulations (special rights) and a say in politics so as to extend their own authority. The introduction of non-hereditary succession to the throne had the aim of installing a weak monarchy, thus consolidating the position of the nobility.

to the seven electors – the archbishops of Cologne, Mainz and Trier, the Count Palatine of the Rhine, the Margrave of Brandenburg, the Duke of Saxony and the King of Bohemia. Whereas the spiritual members of this body acted as arch-chancellors and were given important functions at the coronation, the temporal electors, as in 936, were required to act the parts of lord high steward, marshal, chamberlain and cup-bearer[6]. The decisive period of transition had been the 13th century, when the end of the Staufer dynasty and the interregnum, lasting until 1273, had given the nobility the opportunity of consolidating their concept of the succession to the throne. The unanimous election of Rudolf of Hapsburg had already been preceded in 1256 by the Imperial Diet in Frankfurt transferring the sole right to vote to a body of probably seven electors. As a result, a new king could only be put on the throne by means of an election. But there was another way in which the old positions of the Staufer monarchy had been overtaken by political developments. The unstable ruling conditions during the final years of Frederick II (1212–1250) and the confusions under Conrad IV (1250–1254), followed by the interregnum, had led to the Crown Lands of the Holy Roman Empire (which had originally been the basis of power for the authority of the king) being dramatically reduced in size, taken away or squandered. If they were to be able to rule at all in the Empire, it was vital for the three great royal dynasties in the late Middle Ages – the Hapsburgs, the Wittelsbachs and the Luxemburgs – to build up the power of their families. In other words, they had to consolidate their own sovereignties and weld them together with newly acquired territories to form a unified power bloc. The feudal authority of the German king theoretically continued to exist alongside this and under observance of conventions – indeed, it even became more sophisticated and its institutions better developed. But in spite of this, it could no longer be manorially activated in the face of the territories, and declined to a mere shell. It was only by means of a deliberate policy of building up the power of his dynasty and entering into alliances that the king was now in a position to fulfil the tasks required of him in governing the Empire. It had become impossible to rule the Empire as a whole from the top in the true sense of the word. It was now possible to distinguish between areas that were close to the king, remote from him and open to him, depending on the ruling structure of the area in question. By now it was almost a matter of course for the regions on the middle and lower Rhine to be open to the king, while northern and central Germany were not closely bound to the throne. The process of the division of the king and Empire, which in the 15th century led to a dualism of ruler and estates, proceeded apace – and there was no way of stopping it.

On the other hand, the nobility, acting as an association, were effectively a territory, and this was often confronted by a temporal or spiritual regional prince. This prince or lord, in his turn, had acquired his position by accumulating property and rights. By making sure there were supraregional administrative organizations, he ushered in a change in the status of the territory, to wit the transition from being an association of people to being a territorial area. Territorial sovereignty was developed, and sovereignty over territory was the same as sovereignty over the people living in it. This was a process that is too complicated to be given a brief description. It entailed the sovereign ruler being able to fall back on feudal law (and other methods) in order to consolidate an organizational structure centred on a supreme leader, i.e.

a vertical ruling structure, now that there was no longer any danger of this instrument being reactivated by the king. The final stage was reached when it became possible to integrate the legal system of feudalism into the legal system of the territories – in other words, when feudal ties were no longer related to a person, i. e. the ruler, but to the territory itself. Once this had happened, the land was, by virtue of the constitution of the provincial Estates and the provincial administration, consolidated as it was by feudal law, at last an independent unit in which the dualism between the ruler and the provincial Estates more or less reflected the dualism between the king and the Empire. In view of the particularism thus coming into being, the only way the monarchy could carry on existing was by means of dynamic power politics drawing on its own (crown) reserves. In practice there never has been, never could have been, that type of German king and emperor that at one time was often described as being the forerunner of absolute rule. The delicate circumstances surrounding the entire question of sovereignty and the throne in the Middle Ages always made it necessary to create a balance which certainly might not have had to recognize the legal basis of the claims of other social groups also wanting to participate in power – but they had at least to tolerate this basis in silence. And even today, this silence is still making it difficult for us to understand the Middle Ages.

Notes

1 For more information on this concept, see K. Hauck: "Geblütsheiligkeit" in *Liber Floridus, Festschrift für Paul Lehmann*, St. Ottilien 1950, pp. 187–240.

2 For further information on the martial monarchy, see W. Schlesinger: "Über germanisches Heerkönigtum" in *Das Königtum. Seine geistigen und rechtlichen Grundlagen*, Sigmaringen 1956, pp. 105–141.

3 For reasons of space it is not possible here to go into the problems of the authority exercised by the earls and their constitution. Cf. H. K. Schulze: *Die Grafschaftsverfassung der Karolingerzeit in den Gebieten östlich des Rheins*, Berlin 1973; M. Borgolte: *Geschichte der Grafschaften Alemanniens in fränkischer Zeit*, Sigmaringen 1984, and a reply by H. K. Schulze: "Grundprobleme der Grafschaftsverfassung" in *Zeitschrift für Württembergische Landesgeschichte* 44, 1985, pp. 265–282.

4 On the ambitions of Henry the Lion and a detailed interpretation thereof see J. Fried: "Königsgedanken Heinrichs des Löwen" in *Archiv für Kulturgeschichte* 55, 1973, pp. 312–351.

5 In this case, the right of spoliation was the right of the king to the estate of the deceased clergyman.

6 In the section on provincial law (III 57 § 2) in the "Sachsenspiegel," the "Code of the Saxons," a compendium of mediaeval law compiled by Eike von Repgow (c. 1180- after 1233), it says: "In des keiseres kore scal de erste sin de biscop van Trire, de andere van Megenze, de dridde van Kolne. Under den leien is de erste en deme kore de palenzgreve van'me Rine, des rikes druzte; de andere de marschalk, de hertoge von Sassen; de dridde de kemerere, de markgreve van Brandeborch. De scenke des rikes, de koning van Behemen, de ne hevet nenen kore, umme dat he nicht dudisch n'is." (from *Das Landrecht des Sachsenspiegels*, edited by K. A. Eckhardt, Göttingen 1955, p. 127). Detailed information in E. Boshof: "Erstkurrecht und Erzämtertheorie im Sachsenspiegel" in *Historische Zeitschrift*, Beiheft N. F. 2, 1973, pp. 84–121.

7 Cf. W. Giese: "Der Reichstag vom 8. September 1256 und die Entstehung des Alleinstimmrechts der Kurfürsten" in *Deutsches Archiv 40*, 1984, pp. 562–590.

Forms of Economic Life in the High Middle Ages
by Manfred Groten

Loosening ploughland with a mattock and plough
(c. mid-13th century)
Of all the agricultural implements used in the Middle Ages, there is no doubt that the plough was by far the most important. Two types were used – a primitive plough consisting of a digging stick and handles, and a wheeled plough. The latter was in use at about the time of Christ, but did not become common until the 11th century. It only gradually took over from the digging stick, which could break up the topsoil, but did not turn over the sods of earth.

Agriculture

Mediaeval society was an agricultural society, with at least 90 % of the population working in farming. The peasantry created the food for the nobility, clergy and townsfolk. The vivid language of the Middle Ages called them the feet carrying the body of the people, but their legal position and social standing by no means corresponded to their economic importance. The large majority of the peasants were either serfs or burdened by various kinds of high dues. The Middle Ages distinguished three basic forms of life – prayer, war and work. The first was represented by the clergy and monks, the second by the nobility and knights and the third, apart from craftsmen and merchants, mainly by the peasantry. The last-named were not allowed to carry weapons and so were excluded from chivalry with its promise of social advancement. Only he who could use weapons to defend power could also exercise power. Those who were unarmed could be no more than the object of the power of others. Thus the peasantry that was so typical of the Middle Ages was essentially defined by the creation of a body of professional warriors known as knights.

The ruling class did all it could to control the peasants' way of life so as to keep them firmly within the bounds of their social position, especially when their economic situation noticeably started improving at the height of the Middle Ages. The Chronicles of the Roman and German Emperors, written about the middle of the 12th century, calls upon the highest mediaeval authorities, Emperor Charlemagne and Pope Leo III, to legitimize the legal regulations for the peasantry:

"Now I want to speak about the peasants, the clothes they should wear: they should be black or grey. He (the Emperor) did not allow anything else. Gussets at the side, they befit his way of life. Shoes of cow leather, that is enough. Seven ells of hessian for shirt and trousers. If he has gussets at the front or the back he offends against class privileges. Six days behind the plough and other work suffice. On Sunday he should go to church with his staff in his hand. If he is found to have a sword he must be taken bound to the church fence. Here he must be held fast and flogged. If he is attacked, let him defend himself with a hay fork."

In this text the writer, committed as he was to courtly culture, makes no bones about his disdain for the peasantry. Middle High German literature repeatedly makes clear what courtly conduct is like by comparing it to the uncouth and loutish behaviour of peasants.

To a certain degree, the peasant depicted in literature was only a caricature of reality. Most peasants were unable to afford more than what the rulers would grant them. Mediaeval agriculture generally yielded little, mainly because of the shortage of fertilizer. The profit from wheat, for example, was in the proportion of one part of seeds sown to three parts of grain harvested. Surplus was often devoured by taxes to such a degree that it was but with difficulty that the family could feed itself from what was left. Luxury and splendour were impossible in such circumstances.

The peasants' clothes were usually made of rough cloth. They wore a shirt, short trousers (breeches) and long stockings (hose) and on top of that a tunic fastened at the waist with a belt and usually only going down to the knees so as not to get in the way while working on the fields. The nobility and wealthy citizens, on the other hand, would wear long robes down to the ground and were fashionably adorned, for example with gussets such as those mentioned above. The peasants would protect themselves from the cold and rain by means of an open coat that usually had a hood. Their feet were often only wrapped in cloths or they would wear wooden shoes. The *Bundschuh*, a shoe fastened at the ankle with laces, which was to become the symbol of the rebels during the Peasant Wars (1492–1514), was typical of the peasants' footwear. Simple peasants hardly owned more than one set of clothes, and right up until early modern times the colour could be a typical feature of their estate. It was only wealthy peasants who owned not just everyday clothes, but Sunday attire as well, the splendour of which was a thorn in the flesh of the higher ranks.

The main source of food for the peasants was porridge or millet gruel, which was eaten out of a wooden bowl with a spoon. Unleavened bread was often made. Otherwise rye bread was served. The fine, light-coloured bread made of wheat was regarded as being that of lords of the manor. The peasants also often ate vegetables, such as beans, lentils or peas, and butter, cheese and meat, especially pork and poultry. Strictly speaking, venison was taboo because peasants were not allowed to go hunting. Their banquets were in marked contrast to their frugal daily meals, and preachers never tired of holding forth against the excesses of such occasions.

Peasants were normally bound to a manor. Their feudal lords were the king, the nobility, bishops, convents and monasteries. In its most extreme form, the mediaeval feudal system had three components. The lord was, firstly, the owner of the land tilled by the peasants. This meant that he could charge dues for the use of arable land, meadows and woods. Secondly, he was the supreme judicial authority over the peasants, who were thus beyond the public jurisdiction of the king's representatives, the earls. Since the judicial authority also gave protection, he could charge feudal taxes. The overlord could, thirdly, also be their feudal master if they were serfs. It was particularly regarding this final point that there were the greatest differences, depending on the period, region and ruler.

One thing to be borne in mind is that the term "freedom" has had different meanings at different times. When we talk of freedom today, for example, we are taking such obligations as compulsory schooling, military service and tax liability into account. The Middle Ages had different standards. The extent to which one's life was determined by a feudal master was a decisive criterion.

Serfs with no land of their own were worst off. They were required to serve in the landlord's household, putting their entire working power at his disposal. There was no such thing as freedom for them. As a rule, they were not allowed to marry. They were, however, guaranteed a living and provision for old age. Serfs living in huts in the vicinity of the manor house enjoyed a little more freedom. Serfs cultivating a farmstead of their own had to render certain services for their feudal lords. They also had to pay a poll tax, with special taxes being due in cases of marriage and death.

Work of a peasant (13th century)
The medallions depict two tasks done in rural areas – sowing the grain and harvesting the crops.

Most big manorial estates had been organized as villications since the days of the Carolingian dynasty. A villication consisted of a manor estate with its own economic system and a number of dependent holdings. Either the noble landowner himself lived on the manor estate with his family, or an official usually called a Schultheiss or Meier. The latter was particularly common in the case of very large manor estates made up of several villications. Important monasteries had thousands of peasants living in holdings. The owners of such holdings or *Hufen*, the average size of which is given as 10 hectares, not only had to cultivate their own land but also work for the manor.

We can see what it was like in practice from an article in the land register of Prüm monastery in the Eifel. The article is about Rommersheim farm near the monastery, to which seven *Hufen* manorial land belonged and 30 *Hufen* of land to be cultivated for the landlord. The peasants had to pay the following dues to the monastery – one pig worth 20 pfennigs, one pound of flax, three chickens, 18 eggs, half a load of wine in May and ditto in October, five cartloads of manure, five bundles of tree bark, 12 cartloads of wood, help with baking and brewing, the transport of 50 boards or 100 shigdles for the church roof, a week as a swineherd in the woods, cultivating three acres of the landlord's land three days a week, i.e. ploughing, sowing, harvesting, taking in the harvest, threshing, fencing in the corn fields and meadows, collecting five bushels of corn from Holler (40 km away), guarding the barn, looking after one of the landlord's garden beds. The peasant's wife had to sew trousers. If the abbot visited the estate, the peasants had to join forces to supply four oxen and provide a cart for transport purposes. These demands were originally recorded in 893; the fact that a monk called Caesarius copied them out and annotated them in 1222 shows how tenaciously the feudal landlords clung to their rights over the centuries. Prüm monastery was in this respect, however, extremely conservative. By 1200 most lords of the manor had long given up managing their property themselves and had leased it out to peasants in return for payment in kind or money.

For a number of reasons, the situation of the peasants had considerably improved during the 12th century. A huge growth in the population increased the demand for bread-cereals. The towns were thriving, and here in particular agricultural produce brought good prices. Ploughland was extended to provide food for the growing population by large-scale assarting. Areas that had hardly been developed, such as the Slavonic countries to the east of the German Empire, were systematically colonized. If they were to get peasants to do the hard work all this entailed, the landlords were obliged to offer the settlers particularly favourable legal conditions. This had an effect on all the regions that had long been settled. Here, too, dues and services were reduced to stop the peasants from emigrating to the colonies or towns. One of many examples is provided by a document from Archbishop Philipp of Cologne dating from the year 1171 on changes in the estates of the cathedral capital in Worringen. In order to stem the rural exodus, the taxes for persons over the age of 11 were reduced to 2 pfennigs a year. Six pfennigs were to be paid to the mayor on marriage. If a peasant died, the mayor got either his best horse or, if he didn't own any horses, another animal or an article of clothing. The best linen dress of a dead woman also went to the mayor. A comparison with the Prüm peasants in Rommersheim clearly shows how much freedom the people in Worringen, in the vicinity of the

Windmill
Grain started being ground with the help of wind-mills in the 11th and 12th centuries – a technical innovation Europe owed to the highly developed civilization of Arabia. The picture shows a "post mill."

metropolis of Cologne, had in managing their own affairs. As replacement of loss of income, the mayor was to be paid 6 marks, the cathedral provost 3 marks each year. In order to get this system going and to make sure the payments could be made, 12 peasants first had to collect a total of 70 marks, each according to his wealth – a handsome sum of money which in those days was enough to buy a castle. The foremost peasants in the village were anything but poor.

The final point in the document is particularly interesting because it allows the peasants a certain degree of co-operative autonomy. The withdrawal of the landlords made it possible for the peasants to join together to form a village community, allowing them to regulate their affairs on their own responsibility, according to village law. Such co-operative regulations affected matters like the mutual use of meadows, water and woods (common land), of draught animals (oxen, horses) and better ploughs. It especially stipulated an obligation to conform to certain rules governing the use of land. These were necessary for the three-field system of agriculture that was in common use. For this, all the arable land belonging to a village was divided into three big fields. These were sown either with summer crops or winter crops or left to lie fallow according to a prearranged order, with the use of each field

A medieval village
The village of Rysum in Lower Saxony gives us an excellent impression of what medieval villages looked like. Their layout was mainly circular, with a precisely stipulated system of roads running through them and meeting in the centre. The church was the nucleus of the village.

changing annually. Since so little fertilizer was used, the idea was as far as possible to prevent the soil becoming exhausted. In areas where dairy farming or wine growing predominated, the community had other specific problems to solve.

The appearance of the villages varied from region to region. There were old villages that had grown naturally and now had an uneven layout (nucleated villages). Then there were those that had been established according to a set plan – these were the ribbon-built and the radial villages, the forest villages and the villages in the marshes on the North Sea coast. In some areas, the houses built were larger in size so that the living quarters, barn and the shed for the animals were all under one roof. In others, the various buildings were separate from one another and grouped round the farmyard or even scattered round the land. The construction of pit houses – huts erected in pits in the ground – was very simple.

Comfort in these houses was almost non-existent. An episode in the book of legends by Saint Anno of Siegburg takes us into one such dwelling. There is an open fire burning in the middle of the one and only room and above it there is an earthenware pot with water in it hanging from a hook. A mother leaves her baby, a child not quite a year old, sitting in a hollow dug in the mud floor while she goes out of the house for a short while. At this very moment one of the handles of the pot breaks, and the hot water and the embers from the fire spill all over the child. In this particular instance, St. Anno helps out with a miracle. But such living conditions must have been disastrous for children.

The experience of the uncertainty of life must have had a tremendous influence on the mentality of the peasantry. Peasants were excluded from written culture and so nothing they wrote themselves is extant. The only way we can find out about what they thought, about their religious beliefs is only indirectly – and then it was distorted – in records by the clergy, who scarcely understood or sympathized with the culture of the peasantry. Although every larger village had a parish church, the pastoral care of the inhabitants was frequently dreadful. Matters of religious belief were often only inadequately explained to the peasants. Other social ranks had bishops, abbots, priests, kings, noble gentlemen and ladies presented to them as examples of good behaviour, but in the Middle Ages there was no such thing as a "peasant's saint." On the contrary, peasants were more likely to be suspected of heresy. After all, what else could you think of a peasant's woman who, as the monk called Caesarius of Heisterbach tells us, stole a holy wafer to put into a beehive because her bees weren't doing well – or of another who crumbled up a holy wafer and scattered it over the vegetables to make her plants grow better? Such practices could only be regarded as blasphemous and persecuted as such. And so it is not surprising that in 1233 Pope Gregory IX declared the struggle against the rebellious peasants in Stedinger a crusade.

Rural culture appears in a brighter light in the songs of Neidhart of Reuenthal, who sings about the village festivals that, for a short time, put the greyness of daily life into the background: "Clear away the stools and the chairs! Move the tables to one side! Today we want to tire ourselves out dancing."

Urban Economy

The Middle Ages had taken over the towns as a legacy from the ancient world. It was a legacy they at first didn't really know what to do with. The life of the ancient Germans had scarcely been affected by the towns. For this reason, the heirs of Rome allowed the administrative and economic functions of the towns almost entirely to fall into decay. It was mainly the Church that kept remains of late-antique urbanity going until into the Middle Ages. The bishop resided in town, and his priests looked after religious welfare of the hinterlands and did missionary work there. During the Middle Ages the bishop's church was joined by other collegiate and monastic churches. The clergy and monks of these churches made up a considerable proportion of the urban population. Therefore it was the Church more than anything else that left its mark on early mediaeval towns. These towns presented themselves to the world as a place that was obviously meant to be holy. Examples of such towns with antique traditions in Germany are Trier, Cologne and Mainz. They served as a model for cathedral towns that came into being in the Middle Ages, like Magdeburg, Bremen or Hildesheim.

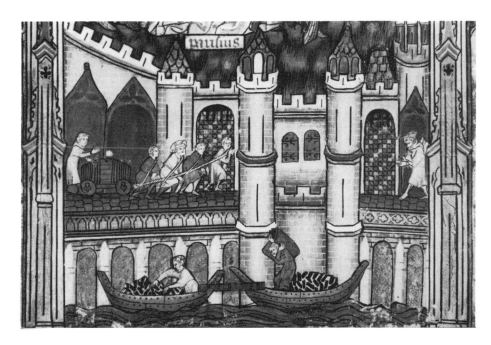

Life in a medieval town (detail from a 14th-century miniature)
In the High Middle Ages, only about 10 % of the population of Germany lived in towns. Since urban areas were important trading and economic centres, a favourable position as far as traffic and transport were concerned was a precondition for the wealth of a town. This is why many towns were built on rivers or major trading routes. Ships were without doubt the most important form of transport for heavy loads. The picture shows men unloading coal ships.

The cathedrals, church foundations and monasteries had to be provided both with articles of daily use and luxury goods. Church-goers from nearby and pilgrims from afar had to be given board and food. And so trade and crafts came to life again in the towns. The bishops surrounded themselves with a retinue of dependent people known as *ministeriales*, who performed important and difficult services and so enjoyed great esteem. *Ministeriales* and merchants were, economically, the biggest and thus most influential groups of people in 11th century towns. Theoretically, these two social groups hardly ever came into contact with one another. Merchants who traded over long distances, and who were generally personally free, earned their wealth on long and dangerous journeys. The *ministeriales*, on the other hand, were unfree; they were responsible for administrative tasks and went to war for the bishops.

The bishops normally exercised full sovereign power over their towns. They were lords of court, and they charged property tax, poll tax and tolls. Walls and towers were within their power. The inhabitants of the towns were bound to the city lords in various ways.

The closest ties were those of bondsmen and bondswomen, and they belonged to the bishop's family. Free town inhabitants, such as merchants and craftsmen, were subject to the city lord's protection and this also involved obligations such as going to court sessions, paying taxes and defending the town from hostile attacks. The demands which were made by the city lord were often felt to be a burden. At the same time, however, there were city laws preventing such claims from turning into arbitrary demands.

City laws had gradually developed from general laws in reply to the needs of many people living together in a confined space. Two examples from the oldest charter of the town of Soest make clear the character of city law:

"§ 31 If someone pledges his house or any other building, and if this is destroyed by fire or any other cause – the new building, if the owner of the building should rebuild it, should act as a pledge, otherwise he must relinquish the ruins and the land to the creditors and the creditor can make no further demands. If, however, the owner lays claim to the ruins, the creditor can ask him to pay the entire debt.

§ 58 If a citzen has taken off his clothes to bathe and at this very moment is summoned to court by a court messenger, he need not follow the summons until he has finished bathing and drying himself."

Townspeople who were used to such legislation strongly objected to the city lords blatantly violating their rights. Uprisings were the result. The first time people revolted was in 1073 in Worms and 1074 in Cologne.

In 1074 Archbishop Anno of Cologne was visited by the Bishop of Münster. When his guest decided he wanted to go home, the archbishop simply confiscated a ship belonging to a merchant from Cologne, threw its freight into the Rhine and chased off the ship's crew. The merchant's son hurried onto the scene with his friends. The young men put the archbishop's servants and the city bailiff to flight. The uprising spread. Anno was besieged in his palace. He fled first to the cathedral and then along a secret passage and out of the city. The archbishop's palace was looted, people were killed, the rebels got ready for a siege. But the archbishop returned with a strong contingent of soldiers and was severe in his punishment.

Scene from the "Jungfrauenspiegel" (late 12th century)
At the peak of the Middle Ages, at least 90 % of the population were involved in agriculture. Work in the fields was extremely difficult, for the peasantry had no special aids to help them. Tools were simple (the picture shows scythes, a rake and a spade), and it was taken for granted that the entire family would muck in. In the picture married women have a head-covering, while the unmarried ones are bare-headed.

Hieronymous Bosch: "The Vagrant" (also known as "The Prodigal Son")
This picture of a pilgrim passing an inn gives us an idea of the way simple people lived; the poverty and uncouthness are particularly striking. The man urinating against the wall of the house is following the custom of the day. The staff carried by the ragged wanderer indicates that it was necessary to be armed as protection against robbers and wild animals.

ILL. PAGE 76:
Saint Francis (wall painting in Pescia, 1235)
The lives of the saints gave people living in the Middle Ages an example to be followed and were a tremendous influence on their way of life on this earth. You turned to the saints in times of need, hoped they would relieve your sufferings in sickness and asked them to intercede on your behalf with the Heavenly Father. The picture shows St. Francis, who can be recognized by his halo and stigmata, speaking to the birds.

ILL. PAGE 77:
Hell (Très Riches Heures of the Duke of Berry, beginning of the 15th century)
The dualism of a heavenly paradise and Hell dominated the concept people living in the Middle Ages had of the world. There were no limits set to the picture painted by the imagination of punishment in Hell. In the centre of the picture we can see Leviathan lying on a red-hot grate and crushing people in his hands. Devils to either side of the grate are fanning the flame to burn the banished souls. In the foreground there are devils cruelly torturing sinners, including clerics.

Persecution of the Jews (from a Hebrew manuscript, c. 1500)
There were a number of Jewish pogroms throughout the entire Middle Ages. The first great wave of persecution set in at the beginning of the First Crusade (1096). The reason for such fanatical hatred of the Jews was not merely the fact that Christians regarded them as being responsible for the crucifixion of Christ. Financial matters also played a part – many Christians had huge debts with Jewish moneylenders. Aggressiveness, coloured with religious ideology, was just the thing to get rid of their economic problem. The Jews very often had little choice but to abandon their possessions and flee.

All these events in Cologne show that the city lord had not expected an uprising and was unable to stifle it at birth. It also makes it clear that the merchants and the archbishop's servants, the *ministeriales*, had not yet joined forces. What is important, however, is the observation that the merchants could already act very resolutely as a community. It was, however, a community that still had to find its true form. When, in his report on the Cologne uprising, a monk called Lampert of Hersfeld expresses his distaste and scorn for the merchants because, after completing business, they talked over wine and good food about warfare and how strong all this made them feel, he only reveals that he has not yet recognized the signs of a new age.

The figure of the town citizen began to clarify early in the 12th century. In the outline of mediaeval society handed down to us, with the three estates of clergy, nobility and peasantry, there is no room for the bourgeoisie. During the Middle Ages, citizens were still having to fight for recognition as an estate. In the 11th century, the Latin word for citizen, *civis*, was still without a clearly defined meaning. All it meant was the people living in any one place – it was possible to talk of the citizens of a village, for example. The term "urban citizen" (*urbani cives*) was not felt to be a superfluous use of two words with similar meanings. It was only gradually that the word "Bürger" (burgaere) came into general use for a "full inhabitant of a city" (Middle High German = burg).

Not every urban citizen was a citizen in the true sense of the word. In many towns, this status was not used for the clergy and monks of ecclesiastical foundations and monasteries. Neither were all laymen regarded as citizens. Only those inhabitants of a town were regarded as belonging to the bourgeoisie who had full rights according to municipal law, most of whom possessed a house and landed property. In many cases, this definition excluded the *ministeriales* of the city overlord, and it never included bondsmen, craftsmen, day labourers, the poor und beggars. The Jewish community in a town also led a life of its own. Thus the bourgeoisie consisted only of a small proportion of city dwellers, but during the high Middle Ages it grew to become the ruling urban group. The town was thus a town of the bourgeoisie, but this certainly did not mean that this social group gained complete control of towns. The city overlords retained part of their old rights. The spiritual institutions, which had had such a strong influence in the early Middle Ages, established associations with rights of their own; urban ecclesiastical lands had the status of immunities, and these were out of bounds for temporal authorities. The castle or palace of the city overlord were also out of bounds for the bourgeoisie. The town houses of nobility and prelates often enjoyed special privileges. As we can see, mediaeval towns seldom presented a homogeneous picture.

At about the same time that Peter Abelard was giving new stress to the human mind as a power of reason, mediaeval man was also becoming conscious of the phenomenon of the town to such an extent that he could now systematically start building new ones. The town, a settlement that hitherto had gradually grown and developed, was now a settlement that could be established in one fell swoop. Historians have drawn up a list of criteria typical of a mediaeval town. The number of inhabitants was of but little importance in the Middle Ages. Cologne was the only city by mediaeval standards (10,000 inhabitants); by the end of the 12th century it covered an area of about 400 hectares and

Slaughtering animals in town
Meat was a regular part of the diet of urban populations in the Middle Ages. Certainly, roast meat tended to be eaten mainly by the privileged patricians, but meat for boiling and offal – trotters, cheek, lungs, liver, kidney and brain – were popular with the lower classes. Tripe was considered a special treat.

probably had some 35,000 inhabitants. Trier and Mainz were counted as being of medium size (2,000 to 10,000 inhabitants). More than 90 % of German towns were small, with between 500 and 2,000 people living in them; from the point of view of the number of inhabitants they hardly differed from villages. A mediaeval town covered a clearly defined area, which had either long been enclosed by a wall to keep it apart from the hinterland or it had a wall built round it in the high and late Middle Ages. The wall made the town into a large castle which, militarily, could be enormously important. The town wall enclosed an area with its own jurisdiction – the territory covered by municipal law. Another characteristic of mediaeval towns was that its citizens possessed a certain degree of autonomy towards the town lords. We shall return to this later. Finally, mediaeval towns were economic, administrative and ecclesiastical centres. Market settlements like Soest or Munich, royal palaces such as Aachen or Frankfurt, and foundations and monasteries like Kempten or Fulda were the embryos of the towns of the high Middle Ages.

One of the earliest towns founded in Germany was Freiburg im Breisgau, founded in 1120 by Conrad of Zähringen. In the foundation deed it says, "Be it known to everyone in the future and now that I, Conrad, set up a market in the year 1120 in a place that is my property, to wit Freiburg. I have decreed that wealthy merchants, who have been called to come here from all over the country, set up and maintain this market. I have therefore bestowed upon each merchant a piece of land in this market for him to build a house thereon according to title and determined that every year on the day of St. Martin each site pay me and my descendants a shilling of public currency in tax. Be it thus known to everyone that at their request and according to their wishes I have granted them the following rights: . . ." The deed addresses the town area and market, municipality and municipal law.

Most towns were founded in Germany in the 13th century. Every prince, no matter how small and unimportant, wanted to be lord of a town, be it for economic or strategic reasons, or simply to show off. In the process, settlements were established scarcely able to develop urban characteristics. Some of them were entirely depopulated by epidemics in the late Middle Ages.

The development of relationships between citizens and town overlords in the high Middle Ages is probably one of the most fascinating and one of the most difficult aspects of urban historiography. The fact that town citizens joined together to form a functioning community was initially the result of outside influences. The court community or the church parish could form such a community. In the 11th century such communities started being filled with new life from within. Typical of the time, and not only in towns, was the urge to establish co-operative associations. It was expressed in the formation of religious brotherhoods, merchants' corporations and craftsmen's guilds. This is also the place to mention the peace movement and the so-called Peace of God for defenceless people and treaties of general peace for whole areas. Municipalities came into being in the towns. Citizens joined forces to form associations, the members of which had to swear to abide by regulations they imposed on themselves.

These associations were a threat to the rights of the town overlords, who, to begin with, understandably enough, were anything but pleased. In Trier in 1161, for example, the associations were outlawed. The Count Palatine of the Rhine wrote: "We herewith give notice to your community that my lord, the archbishop of your town, has lodged a bitter complaint with the Emperor and the entire court because you have created a community with new customs and unusual rights against his honour and the old rights."

There were violent uprisings in several towns. But gradually the town overlords realized that this citizens' movement could no longer be suppressed. There were compromises between the rulers and the associations. The town overlords granted rights that, little by little, were often extended. In the late Middle Ages, the most powerful of the towns had de facto managed to drive their overlords completely out of the town walls. In most towns, a sign of the acquired autonomy was the town seal, possession of which showed the municipality to be a body incorporated under its own law. The oldest town seals in Germany were given to the municipalities of Trier, Cologne and Mainz in the first third of the 12th century.

Initially, the leaders of the municipalities were men who had previously held prominent positions in the town. They saw themselves as being the most distinguished people in town, as being a cut above the rest *(meliores, optimates, primores)*. In many German towns there were bodies of jurors chaired by the town overlord or his judges, and their task was to pass judgement. Another of their tasks, of course, was to lead the bourgeois community. In earlier days, the town overlord had appointed the jurors at his own discretion, but it now became customary for the jurors to fill vacant positions as they saw fit. The community had

The town of Carcasonne
This view of the French town of Carcasonne, with its excellently preserved medieval town centre, is an impressive illustration of the important function of the town wall; it protected the inhabitants from hostile attacks and was thus of great military importance; at the same time, however, it also limited urban expansion to the area within the walls. During the 13th century, various quarters came into being that were associated with individual social groups.

Cloth dyers at work

As early as the 12th century and more particularly in the 13th century, guilds, associations of artisans of like profession, were established. There were three main reasons for the development of the guild system. Protection from overwhelming rivalry, to ward off illegal competition, mutual procurement of raw materials and equipment – these were economic reasons. Protection of a trade's good name and safeguarding the honest and reliable production of goods – these were professional and ethical factors of no mean significance. Finally, there was a religious element, which was manifested in the fact that each guild revered its own saint.

little influence on such practices. It was inevitable that this should result in nepotism, and in due course opposition to it grew. Arguments and fights among the town inhabitants sooner or later led to the formation of town councils in most towns, the seats of which were distributed proportionately among the various groups of the population, such as jurors, *ministeriales*, merchants, craftsmen. Shifts within the social structure of a town could lead to changes to the council constitution. The town hall became the centre of interest of the townsfolk. It was often allocated a representative parish church. The town council was led by the mayor, who was normally in office for only a limited period. We must be careful not to see the constitution of the council in a wrong light, for it was not a democratic instrument. Only town citizens with full civic rights were entitled to vote. Certain families deemed "suitable" – i.e. families who could afford to spend time on political matters – were eligible to be elected to sit on the council, a task which, after all, brought no financial gain. The council ruled over "its" citizens in very much the same way as any other authority. It is not for nothing that the literature of the day speaks of the "lords" of the council.

In the first place, it was the *ministeriales* and merchants who were on the council. The proportion of *ministeriales* in the leading stratum of society has been particularly well examined in the case of Trier, but they are unlikely to have played a lesser role in other places. Let us take as an example a juror, one Ordulf von Oeren (died 1311), scion of a family known since the 12th century; he paid for the convent of St. Catherine to be moved into the town and gave generous presents to the nuns; other members of his family had assets, income and rights in more than 30 other places outside Trier. *Ministeriales* led a very chivalrous life; they had coats of arms, owned expensive armour, equipment and horses, lived in town in solid stone houses or towers, but very often also had country residences in which to spend the summer. They mainly lived off the profits from their assets, but were also involved in wholesale trade. Frequently they were involved in the bullion business, minting and money deals. In this respect they differed very little from leading merchant families, as we shall see shortly.

For a while, German historians thought the merchants had played a decisive role in the rise of the mediaeval class of citizens – a view that has since been revised. Nevertheless, the importance of the merchants for urban development must not be underestimated. Only those merchants not away on long trading journeys, however, could influence events in the towns. Long-distance traders were often away from home for years at a time.

The life led by these men forms the background for a drastic story told in The Cambridge Songs (early 11th century): A townsman from Constance goes on a long trade journey, is shipwrecked and doesn't return home for two years. In the meantime, his wife has been passing the time of day with charlatans and young men and confronts her husband with an illegitimate child. She tells him that while she was walking in the hills she drank melted snow and this made her pregnant. The merchant pretends to believe her story. Another five years later he again goes on his travels, taking the "snow child" with him. He sells the child to a merchant on the other side of the sea for 100 pounds of silver and returns home, where he tells his wife that the "snow child" melted in the heat of the south. The slave trading hinted at here was a deplorable reality in mediaeval Europe.

A medieval apothecary
Compared to the present day, medical care in the Middle Ages was completely inadequate. Knowledge of disease, its causes and treatment mainly came from the medical writings of the Greeks and Arabs. All doctors ever did was to listen to a patient's chest, let blood or give him pills and potions. The Italian town of Salerno was a centre of medicine in the 12th and 13th centuries and had the reputation of having extremely good doctors.

The trading routes used by long-distance traders – roads, rivers, sea routes – covered the whole of Europe and the Near East. In the late Middle Ages, North German merchants were organized as the Hanseatic League, and they travelled to France, England, Scandinavia and Russia. The Rhine and Danube were the arteries of long-distance trading in continental Europe. Other trading routes went to Italy and, above all, to Venice, or to the four important sites of mediaeval trade fairs in the Champagne – Troyes, Provins, Lagny-sur-Marne and Bar-sur-Aube. In the main, German merchants were only indirectly involved in trade with the Orient.

It would be impossible to give a detailed list of the goods that were traded. Cologne traders took wine to England and brought back wool. Swords from Cologne are given high praise in French epic poetry. Pingsdorf ceramics from near Cologne were taken up to Trondheim and all the way to Novgorod. In return, it was possible to buy amber, honey, wax and Russian furs in Cologne. Monk Caesarius of Heisterbach tells of two Cologne merchants who were commissioned to buy a polar bear skin in Norway to make an altar-cloth. Nor did the people of the day make any bones about trading with relics. According to a report dating back to 1181, only miraculous powers were able to prevent the skeleton of one of the 11,000 virgins being sold to Huy. Rare spices like aniseed, ginger, pepper, cloves, saffron, cinnamon were imported by the sack, and huge quantities of silk, purple cloth, precious stones and medicines were also brought to Europe. Goldsmith's products and other artefacts as well as metal ores were transported across half of Europe. Cloth, grain, fish and salt were needed in large quantities. Herds of cattle and horses were driven over long distances.

Council meeting (from a Swiss chronicle, beginning of the 16th century)
Struggles and disputes among the citizens of the towns gave rise to the formation of town councils headed by the mayor. The council constitution stipulated the principles governing the administration of a town and controlled relations in the community. The right to vote was limited to full citizens, while only the members of a few families were considered eligible for election to the council. The rule of the town councillors was no less hard than that of the princely lords; thus contemporary sources speak respectfully of the "lords of the council."

Obviously, not all these transactions were above board. Caesarius, the monk mentioned above, tells of two Cologne merchants who admitted quite freely at confession that in their profession they would not be able to get by without lies and perjury. Greed for profit was regarded as being sinful, and usury, i.e. moneylending with interest, was even classified as a deadly sin. To begin with, the only people who were willing to risk such transactions, apart from Jews, were Lombards (North Italians) and citizens from Cahors in southern France. In about 1200 a Lombard named Petrus is mentioned as living in Cologne.

Many a merchant tried to pacify his bad conscience by donating generously to the Church. It is again Caesarius of Heisterbach who gives us a good example of this. A wealthy Cologne merchant gave the canons of the college of St. Apostel a shipload of stones for them to build a church. In this manner he was hoping to make up for the burden of his sins – a truly mercantile thought. Other merchants, fearing for their souls, donated hospitals, chapels, altar-panels, liturgical books and vessels and ecclesiastical vestments. A man's debts were all settled on his death bed, deceptions atoned, requiem masses arranged and the poor ordered to be fed. There are several reports of nothing but toads being found in a wealthy merchant's money boxes after his death. Such stories are meant to remind the world of how transient and useless wordly goods are. Some merchants ended their lives in a monk's habit. St. Norbert, the founder of the order of the Premonstratensian Canons, is said to have occasioned the spontaneous entry of several Würzburg citizens to the clergy by restoring a blind man's sight in 1126. The younger sons and daughters of merchant's families were often sent to monasteries and convents.

In the 12th century, wealthy merchants started adopting a lifestyle that was reminiscent of that of knighthood, and by the 13th century their way of life was decidedly chivalrous. On the oldest German seal awarded to a citizen, that of the Cologne juror Wilhelm vom Markt (awarded 1226), the holder of the seal is still in civilian clothing, with a long robe and a fashionable fur-lined coat – and unarmed. Seals dating back to the second half of the 13th century depict shields. Members of families that were originally bourgeois started being knighted from about that time. Thus the lower nobility and merchantry coalesced. At the end of the 12th century, Gerhard Unmaze from Cologne was a typical example of this synthesis of bourgeoisie and chivalry. On the one hand, Gerhard was an archiepiscopal *ministerialis* and, for a time, a sub-bailiff and tax collector. On the other hand, he was also a large-scale financier, juror and mayor. The poet Rudolf of Ems probably based his poem "Gerhard the Good" on him. The ironic reference to the courtly ideal of "mâze," meaning "discretion," contained in Gerhard's surname is typical of the mentality of townspeople, who had to use such additional names to distinguish themselves from others of the same name.

The artisans were below the merchants in the social hierarchy of the urban population. Artisans possessed varying degrees of wealth, depending on the trade and size of the business. Furriers, goldsmiths and wool weavers were scarcely less wealthy than merchants, while cobblers and linen weavers could often only just about get by on their earnings. In the big cities, the trades were extremely specialised. In 1149, blanket weavers are mentioned in Cologne, and in 1225 lawn weavers.

Following the practice of the day, artisans joined together to form craft organizations, which were usually called guilds. The oldest deed of a guild is dated 1149 and comes from Cologne. It states: "Be it not concealed from believers of all stations, in the future and now, that some men, lovers of justice, to wit Reinzo, Wilderich, Heinrich, Everold and others who practise this craft, have founded a fraternity of blanket weavers in the pious hope of eternal life." The religious overtone, which at first may seem out of place in this context, was by no means without its justification in the Middle Ages. The guilds were not merely concerned with the economic interests of their members, but were a community embracing all aspects of life. Their members helped each other in life and prayed for the soul of their dead brothers.

A lot of the artisans sold their wares at market. The impressions made by mediaeval markets on the eyes, ears and nose is shown by a deed dating from 1269 and describing a striking detail at market: a butcher's stall is mentioned, and next to it a particular kind of torture instrument – a chair from which culprits could be shoved so that they would land "where at certain times whole stomachs of oxen, cows and sheep are sold"!

The great majority of townsfolk were poor – servants, labourers, beggars. A lot of these people had come from the surrounding regions after running away from their masters. The anonymity of the town gave them cover and shelter and, after a while, liberty from old ties. The lowest strata in particular must have dominated the general picture afforded by the streets, for the wealthy probably only appeared in public in force on special occasions. The poor thronged through the dirty streets on foot – and high society only ever went anywhere, even short distances, on horseback. Since there was very little poor relief, there were always beggars hanging around churches, the market and the houses of the rich. They were particularly numerous at processions or if a prince or the emperor came to town.

The big towns, the cities, always took the lead as far as social developments were concerned. There were already academically trained doctors and lawyers in Cologne in about 1200. It was here that new religious movements got going, such as that of the Beguines and Beghards and then the begging orders. Heretics, too, were given attention. Cathari from Flanders were already being burnt at the stake in Cologne in 1163. The urban way of life obviously encouraged criminality. There is a record of jurors in Cologne sentencing a man called Arnold "because he played at dice and inflicted three wounds on a beautiful woman (i.e. a prostitute)." Scenes such as these had already been seen by Caesarius of Heisterbach during his youth in Cologne. "Theobald was addicted to wine and dice and well-known as a buffoon all over town. I often saw him walking along the streets naked."

When Isabella, the sister of King Henry III of England, stopped at Cologne on her way to her betrothed, Emperor Frederick II, the reception she was given must have been an uplifting spectacle. Roger of Wendover described it thus: "When news of her arrival became known, 10,000 townspeople dressed in festive clothes and carrying flowers and palm twigs streamed towards her. Those sitting on Spanish horses spurred them on, while breaking each other's sticks and lances in jousting." Matthäus Paris, a later chronicler, added: "There were also ships which, by means of clever tricks, seemed to sail by on dry land, pulled by horses hidden beneath silken covers. And there were clerics sitting on these ships, who, to the mellow sound of organs, were melodiously singing songs the amazed audience had never heard before."

Cologne town seal (13th century)
Most German towns were founded in the 13th century. Apart from economic or strategic considerations, it was very often nothing more than petty provincial princes showing off that gave rise to a town being built. In this way, towns came into being that were scarcely able to develop urban features. On an average, towns had about 500–1000 inhabitants. Cologne, with almost 35,000 inhabitants, was the only German city.

Seal of the Cologne citizen Wilhelm vom Markt (1226)
After about 1325, more town citizens tended to have their own seal. In this way they manifested their claim to social equality with the nobility, whose lifestyle town patricians tried to imitate.

The Age of Christendom: A View of the Life of Christians in the High Middle Ages
by Thomas Ruster

Chimera on Notre Dame in Paris (c. 1250)
The mysterious gnomes, gargoyles and demons on Gothic cathedrals are clear proof that medieval Christians feared dark powers no less than their heathen ancestors. Many Christian customs and festivals at that time were essentially a continuation of pre-Christian rituals.

Our language has a word that has been doing well for itself in this modern day and age. It has climbed the ladder of success and popularity and covers a number of situations. The word is "society." It more or less means the entirety of the human race, all the human beings we have dealings with or whom we can see. In the Middle Ages, however, no one spoke of society, but rather of "Christendom" (christianitas). This was because in those days everybody people knew was Christian. To be sure, somewhere, there were pagans (e.g. Normans), people whose faith was not in accordance with established doctrines (the Saracens, for example) and Jews. But they lived a long way off, beyond the borders of the country or, in the case of the Jews, in ghettos. The average person hardly ever set eyes on them. Mediaeval "society" was Christendom. For this reason it is not easy to say much about the life of Christians in the Middle Ages. To do so, it would be necessary to describe the way people of that age lived – the life of people dominated from birth to death by Christianity and the Church, people living in hope of a life after death in the community of the saints. Let us try to look at the life Christian people led in the Middle Ages.

1. Three Appeals – Three Signs of the Times

"Give me the Lord, give me the Lord!" cried a sick lad who in the 13th century had mistakenly been given unconsecrated bread as a cure. This lad was not only able to tell an unconsecrated wafer from a consecrated one simply by its taste or appearance; he also firmly believed that the body of Jesus Christ was a strong and effective medicine for his illness. Spirit and body had for him joined to form a single unit. For people in the Middle Ages, spiritual matters, especially those connected with church sacraments, were manifest, miraculous and real. The down-to-earth Romans were baffled by the earthy and materialistic piety which had arisen in Germany under the influence of the Germanic-Franconian spirit. As far as we are concerned, the borderline between magic and belief is blurred. Some people were given the privilege of seeing consecrated bread "crystalline and with the sunlight shining through it"; others, after receiving Holy Communion, were given the grace to float a foot above the ground. The oxen of a peasant busy at his ploughing came to an amazed halt in front of a pyx thrown into a furrow by thieves. Anyone who dropped the body and blood of the Lord onto the ground had to do penance for forty days. When the communion of the sick was carried through the streets, everyone who heard the tinkling of the accompanying bell fell to their knees. There is also the story of a priest who retained the body of Christ in his mouth after communion so as to get a woman to succumb to his will by kissing her. There are many accounts of miracles: once, when a host fell onto the ground in St. Columba's in Cologne, "the hardness of the stone beneath it disappeared and a circle and letters appeared in it." There are many such

Lenten sermon (mid-15th century)
Penance was done at least once a year, during
Lent; the weeks prior to Easter were reserved for
penances, which were often considerable. The
penitent was obliged to avoid such foods as meat,
milk, cheese, and marital intercourse, dances and
carousing.

examples. The tenets of mediaeval piety were firmly based on a belief in
the all-embracing unity of divine, sacramental and earthly reality.

"Rome, Rome," cried a young woman of bourgeois family in Flanders, who had just fled from the altar at her wedding because she did not
want to marry the man intended for her. It was not that she was hoping
to find a better husband in Rome. Rather, she was calling upon ecclesiastical law, which, since the 12th century, had recognized marriage by
consent, according to which no one, not even women, could be forced to
marry against their will. It was, however, common for a woman to have
her husband chosen by her family, and so a young couple very often did
not meet until the wedding day. In the first collection of universal
ecclesiastical laws published in 1140, Gratian the monk declared the
consent of both parties to be a condition of marriage; he also said that
love should be the foundation of marriage and not the economic and
political interests of the people concerned – a somewhat unusual statement for that time. Does this mean that women enjoyed the same rights
as men? No one went that far, but all the same – "Eve was not created
from Adam's feet, and therefore she must not be kicked about. She was
not made from his head, and so she must not rule." This mediaeval
saying speaks for itself. It shows how Church ethics increasingly influenced areas of public life and tried to mould them according to Christian
belief. For example, it was forbidden to charge interest for financial
transactions, the idea being to follow the example of the Bible and put a
stop to moneylending and fraud. The Bible was often referred to when it
came to dealing with difficult legal and financial matters; ecclesiastical
jurisdiction covered such matters as adultery and perjury, the return of
stolen property and laws of inheritance. The field of science was particularly imbued with the idea that the Christian spirit should pervade the
whole of reality. Philosophy, at one time the queen of the sciences, was
degraded to be the handmaiden of theology; theologians like Albertus
Magnus (1200–1280) and Roger Bacon (1220–1292) set out to explore the
nature of human feelings and the laws of living together. There was
nothing in this age of Christendom not open to the influence of the
Church and religious belief. Thus public and social life was always and
inseparably Church/ecclesiastical life as well.

The habit of St. Francis of Assisi (1181–1226)
This habit, made of undyed woollen material,
clearly reflects the ideals of St. Francis – austere
poverty following the example of Christ. St. Francis founded the first mendicant orders in about
1210 to reform monasticism from the very roots.
The reform was based both on the renunciation of
individual and corporate ownership of property
and on pastoral involvement.

"It is God's will!" – for over a century this was the battle cry of
Crusade preachers in the Christian West, and innumerable people followed their call. Beggars and swindlers, the mob from the streets and
young men from wealthy families, priests and knights, kings and
emperors – they all set off to snatch the Holy Land out of the clutches of
heathens. In all, there were seven Crusades, and enthusiasm, particularly for the first one (1096–1099), knew no bounds: Now that battle was
to be done against the pagans, righteous anger was also directed against
infidels at home. Merciless pogroms against the Jews in Mainz, Worms,
Speyer and other towns initiated a century of cruelty, contempt for
human beings and senseless bloodshed scarcely equalled in history.
"Why did the heavens not darken, why did the stars not cease to shine,
or the sun and the moon, why did they not grow dark in the vault of the
heavens when 1100 holy persons were murdered and slaughtered on one
day, so many little children and babes in arms who had done no wrong
nor sinned, so many poor and innocent souls! – Eternal Father, how can
you look upon this?" demanded a Jewish chronicler in Mainz in 1096. "It
is God's will" – the hordes surged on through the Christian empires of
Hungary and Byzantium and "no one ever thought of buying what he
needed, everyone lived from murder and pillage as best he could." The
uncontrolled mobs were soon on the point of collapse from exhaustion,
hunger and battle; the Holy Land was only reached by the better
organized armies of knights, who in spite of huge losses conquered
Jerusalem on 15 July 1099 after a five-week siege. Streams of blood were
shed – the horses were fetlock-deep in blood, and other reports talk of
the horses wading knee-deep in the blood of the Saracens. A Christian
kingdom was then set up in Jerusalem to the accompaniment of murder,
looting and rape. It lasted for not quite 100 years.

The other Crusades were less "successful" than the first one, but no
less cruel. The Second Crusade (1147–1149), initiated by Bernhard of
Clairvaux, was a failure and only resulted in Lisbon being conquered
from the Moors. The Third Crusade (1189–1191), a gigantic undertaking
under Emperor Frederick Barbarossa, collapsed while still on the road
after the Emperor had drowned while bathing in the River Saleph. Pope
Innocent III put the full weight of his power behind the Fourth Crusade
(1202–1204). The crusaders, who wanted to be taken across the sea on
Venetian ships, first had to pay their debts by destroying Venice's trade
rival Zara in Istria before – how tragicomical history can be – they turned
to the matter of laying waste the East Roman city of Constantinople. The
cause had been quarrels concerning the succession to the Greek throne.
The Crusade against their Christian brothers turned into an unprecedented plundering expedition.

In retrospect, it is now hardly possible to understand the reasons
why these multitudes of people took part in the Crusades. Was it the
papal promise of remission from sins in the after-life for everyone
participating in armed pilgrimages? Was it the prospect of loot and
material gain? Were the Crusades an ideal activity for knights who had
been made practically redundant by changes in warfare when, to crown
it all, their profession was given religious legitimation? Were the princes
trying to consolidate their internal power by ousting their rivals? Did the
Church want to become the leading power in the West and thus
emphasize its claim to universal sovereignty? Probably a little of all these
motivated the people concerned. And what part was played by religious
attitudes?

One thing that must be realized is that there was virtually no hindrance to Christians pilgrimaging to Jerusalem, even when the town was under Moslem rule. Yet a saint like Bernhard of Clairvaux devoted the entire power of his gift of oratory to pleading for the cause of the crusades. Saint Francis, on the other hand, preferred to go personally to the Egyptian sultan so as to convert him, not with weapons, but with words (1219). He was given a friendly reception and allowed to preach at length. Religious mania and despair at the failure of previous military efforts are reflected in the mad undertaking of the Children's Crusades which, under the leadership of two boys, one from Cologne and one from Vendômois in France, set off in 1212 to conquer the Holy Land with divine assistance alone. They were joined by tens of thousands of children. The journey was hard and full of privations; those that survived it were taken as slaves or put into brothels in the port towns of the Mediterranean. Very few returned home.

And the outcome of the Crusades, which were organized by the Church, politicians and the people of the Middle Ages? Historians estimate the dead at 22 million.

Our three glimpses of the mediaeval world of religious belief and the Church show us an enthralling picture full of contradictions. What sort of age was this – an age in which piety and cruelty, scholarship and superstition, an open humanitarian spirit and religious mania were able to exist side by side in the name of the same beliefs and in the bosom of the same Church? Very often the only information our school and history books can give us in the chapter headed "The Middle Ages" concerns the struggle for power between pope and emperor. All we see is the tip of the iceberg. This struggle was fought on various levels of power between numerous opponents in the investiture conflict, which

Day of Judgement (tympanon over the princes' portal in Bamberg cathedral)
"And before him shall be gathered all nations: and he shall separate them one from another, as a shepherd divideth his sheep from the goats: and he shall set the sheep on his right hand, but the goats on the left. Then shall the King say unto them on his right hand, Come, ye blessed of my Father, inherit the kingdom prepared for you from the foundation of the world..." (Matthew 25:32–34)

Poor Clares at table
For women, convent life was often the only way of escaping from male domination. A large number of female orders were founded at the beginning of the 13th century, such as that of the Benedictine nuns or the Dominican nuns. The order of St. Clare, or the "Little Sisters of Poverty," was founded by St. Francis of Assisi in 1212.

climaxed in the dispute between Pope Gregory VII and Emperor Henry IV and was settled in 1122 in the Concordat of Worms. The matter at hand was the *libertas ecclesiae,* the liberty of the Church or, to be more precise, the right of the Church to make appointments of its own choice. But the temporal rulers also made claim to this right for, after all, it was they who provided the finance for maintaining the Church. In addition, many of the prelates, such as the archbishops of Cologne, Trier and Mainz, were also princes with temporal authority. Thus the double interest in their investiture was certainly justified. If the question of their investiture was to be settled, then the whole question of power also had to be settled. As far as this was concerned, the Church – in the age of Christendom – had little difficulty in showing that all authority comes from God and that therefore the pope, Christ's vicar, was entitled to the highest authority on earth. True, the "Two Sword Doctrine" acknowledged that a spiritual and a temporal sword were necessary to rule the world, but the popes never tired of emphasizing that the spiritual sword was of higher rank and therefore had the duty of ruling over the temporal sword in the name of the Lord. Ambitious popes like Gregory II (1073–1086) and Innocent III (1198–1216) saw themselves as temporal rulers and granted land as benefices to kings they favoured. An extended legate system put them in a position to control the domestic politics in the empires; neither did they have any qualms about using excommunication and damnation as a form of coercion in political matters. Although they very often had real power on their side, the temporal rulers were not easily able to escape from the arguments of the pope because they, too, saw themselves as ruling by divine grace and, whenever possible, sought confirmation of their position by the pope. What was right for popes and emperors was also right for local rulers. Archbishop Anno II of Cologne (1056–1075), who was also a prince of the Empire, was not only active and influential in imperial politics; he also interfered with the rights of the townspeople so drastically that once, after he had arbitrarily confiscated a merchant's ship, there was an uprising and the bishop's palace was attacked. In spite of all these struggles and conflicts, the unity of Middle Age Christendom is clearly visible – a unity based on the unquestioning respect and power of temporal and spiritual leaders, based on a belief embracing all people as far as the ends of the earth, controversial only in its practical organization, that is, the way sovereign authority was assigned in the struggle between spiritual and temporal dignitaries.

And yet – and this is what really gives Christendom in the Middle Ages its proper colours – there was resistance from many sides to a spiritual and temporal unity which, in the final analysis, was only motivated by power politics. No mean number of men and women, seeing the secularization of the Church as a huge aberration of the spirit of Jesus Christ, demanded a return to true spirituality and the gospel. The reform of monasticism, centred on the Benedictine order at Cluny in Burgundy (from A.D. 909 onwards), tightened up the strict rules of Benedict, the founder of the order, and committed the monks to spending most of the day in prayer and at worship. Their work, in numerous Benedictine monasteries, was reformatory in character and continued until well into the 11th and 12th centuries. After the decline of Cluny (the result of too much accumulated wealth) it was primarily the monasteries of Hirsau in the Black Forest, Cîteaux (Cistercians) and Clairvaux (Bernhard of Clairvaux, 1115–1153) which inspired believers by their ascetic zeal, their love of handicrafts and the severity of their regulations. One courageous young woman was the abbess Hildegard of Bingen (1098–1179); she openly preached in Cologne and elsewhere against the corruption and power-madness of the clergy and nevertheless became a popular advisor to many prelates and princes. Francis of Assisi (1181–1226), the founder of the mendicant orders, went even further: Himself the son of a wealthy merchant draper, he lived a simple life following the example of Jesus Christ and His apostles, and expected others to do so. He saw property, power and prestige as a contradiction of the gospel. Even during his life, he and his sister Clare had a huge following, many of them young people.

On the other hand, there were attempts by temporal rulers to emancipate themselves from the dominance of spiritual authority. One example is the German emperor Frederick II (1215–1250). He was a highly talented, versatile and well-educated prince, an enthusiastic architect and patron of poetry; on the island of Sicily he established a form of state that was largely free of the influence of the Church. His scepticism, his free dealings with Jews and Saracens and his moral independence were a cause of umbrage with many of his contemporaries. He, too, remained loyal to the Church, but in many ways his Sicilian state anticipated the modern, secular and lay form of government.

2. Faith and Money. The Daily Life of Christians

The history of the big names in the ecclesiastical and secular worlds, which is usually what history books tell us about, sheds light on this period – but they also throw a dark shadow over the life of ordinary people. What was life within the bosom of the Church like for people in the Middle Ages?

Whatever else Christians in the Middle Ages were, they were not the Sunday Christians that are common nowadays. Their life in any given place was always a life in one particular church parish, and the sum total of these two elements made up everyone's daily life. A christening not only made the person concerned into a child of God; it also announced that he or she belonged to the parish in which the font was. From this moment on, this parish church was responsible for the sermons that person heard, for their confession, marriage, communion of the sick and funeral. It was to this parish church that fees for church ceremonies had to be paid, and so it was very much in the interests of the parish priest not to lose control of believers. At the christening, the first act of religious instruction for the children was for them to be read the creed – by custom in the 13th century, to the boys in Greek and the girls in Latin. In spite of this subtle difference, Christians had but little knowledge of matters of faith. Complaints that the faithful "had to get by with no knowledge of religion and faith" were voiced regularly, and priests were exhorted to take instruction of the laity much more seriously. All told, it was generally thought sufficient for people to know the creed and the Lord's Prayer and how they should live. Church life was not focussed on the word, but on the sacraments. The importance of the Eucharist has already been mentioned. Prior to the 11th century, penance was done at least once a year – before Lent, so that this period was available for penitential exercises, which were often considerable. There is an account of a nun from St. Mary's in Cologne who as penitence

Arm reliquary of St. Elizabeth (Western Germany, c. 1240)
Elizabeth of Thuringia (1207–1231) was highly revered because of her life of privation and charitable deeds. She founded a hospital near Marburg and devoted herself entirely to the care of the poor and sick. According to medieval reports, there were a number of miraculous cures at her grave in the church of St. Elizabeth in Marburg.

Monk and nun in the stocks
The strict rules for members of religious orders stipulated that they renounce all worldly pleasures. But in the Middle Ages, celibacy was not taken all that seriously. In spite of repeated admonishments by the pope, most priests lived with a woman, sometimes in return for the payment of a fee – and this was officially allowed by the bishops. The picture here – found in the margin of a book – was meant to be a deterrent for monks unable to resist the temptations of the flesh.

is said to have voluntarily recited the whole of the Book of Psalms (i.e. 450 psalms) three times a day for eleven years – once stretched out on the ground, once kneeling and once standing. As the list of sins was later extended and became more detailed, the open confession of one's sins to the priest was regarded as being the true act of penance and other penitential exercises were no longer required. Confession was in the pre-Easter period; Easter confession and communion were one of the Church commandments from 1215 onwards. After confession it was customary to give the priest a present, but the priest was on no account to spare sinners because of the gifts. The consumption of meat, milk, cheese and the like was strictly forbidden during Lent, likewise marital intercourse, dancing and carousing.

Public marriage in church was not customary in the Middle Ages, for the Church regarded marriage vows made in the presence of the families, together with the handing over of the dowry, as legally valid. It was, however, an old custom to pray for a woman before she gave birth to a child and, after confinement, to church her – i.e. celebrate reconciliation with her – because the Old Testament said she was impure. It was not until later that Pope Innocent III clearly stated that women were "burdened by no sin" because of giving birth. In the Middle Ages, marriage was regarded as being "beautiful and agreeable in the eyes of the Lord," but people also clearly saw "that the countless serpents of worldly care may arise from it" (Elizabeth of Schönau, 1125–1164).

Extreme unction in conjunction with communion of the sick was a solemn act in which all the priests in the village participated if possible. Although anointment did not take place until shortly before death, its original meaning was that of healing the body, symbolized in the healing power of oil. The priest would anoint the painful parts of the body as well as certain places on the neck, throat, between the shoulders, on the chest, near the sensory organs – if necessary he would perform the act of anointment on seven consecutive days. A prayer would be said to drive out the devil, the benediction pronounced, the "effective medicine of the flesh and blood of Christ" administered. If, in spite of all this, death ensued, people living in the house and neighbours gathered round to keep the deathwatch. The time before and after death gave mediaeval piety great scope for activity. Praying fraternities were established, which met to give mutual support at times of death. The guilds of artisans and merchants were also religious communities which prayed for their dead and had mass read. This was more than just standing by someone during the last hours of their life; rather, people feared both the interference of the devil in the deceased's journey to the afterlife and at the Day of Judgement. When the angels accompanied St. Martin to the afterlife, there was such fierce fighting with the devil that the singing of the heavenly hosts stopped for a while. In this case, the prayers of the faithful and masses for the dead were invaluable. The suffering of the deceased in purgatory could be shortened with the help of prayers and mass. Mediaeval books of the dead show us how much was paid for the prayers of the brothers and sisters (i.e. monks and nuns) and masses for the dead. Most convents, monasteries and big churches were largely built from the money for masses for the dead.

Apart from the sacrament of extreme unction, the Church also offered the sick and suffering other means of healing – the miraculous relics of saints stored under the altars of the churches. There were innumerable accounts of cures by the power of the saints and they would

Ratekau (Romanesque village church, seen from the south)
Life in the Middle Ages was dominated by the Church to a degree that is hardly conceivable nowadays. Baptism not only made the child into a child of God, but also meant it belonged to the church holding the font. People were not only dependent on the parish church for matters like sermons, marriages, communion of the sick and funerals; they also had to pay church tithes and fees for religious deeds by the church.

Berthold of Regensburg (from a 15th-century manuscript)
Between 1250 and 1272, the Franciscan monk Berthold of Regensburg travelled through southern Germany, Bohemia, Moravia and Thuringia, calling people to repent. Berthold was doubtless the most colourful of the itinerant preachers roving through the entire Empire in the 13th century. He reproached the followers crowding to his sermons in droves for their sinful misdemeanors, painted a vivid picture of the tortures awaiting them in hell and admonished them to leave the path of sin and lead a life pleasing to God.

spread like wild-fire. It was therefore well known which saints were particularly effective for which particular complaint. If the wise women, doctors and barber-surgeons could no longer be of help, the next step was often a long and expensive pilgrimage to the sacred relics to get help by means of prayer and pious gifts. Many people returned home cured, but not before increasing the wealth of the place of pilgrimage. And so, hand in hand with the pilgrimage business, there was a large-scale chase after relics. They were "found" (often during the crusades), stolen, seized, broken up into little pieces, doubled and traded – all to multiply the fame and income of the churches back home. In many respects, the mediaeval pilgrimage business corresponded to the mass tourist industry of the 20th century. The *Canterbury Tales* by Geoffrey Chaucer (c. 1340–1400) show how entertaining and educational such a pilgrimage (in that case to the shrine of Thomas Becket in Canterbury) could be. Such journeys often took months, and the pilgrim certainly didn't just talk of religious matters and tales of the saints. A thirst for travel and pious desires, hope for help and getting to know foreign parts – a pilgrimage served to satisfy all these wishes and more besides.

It has been estimated that in 13th century Germany one person in nine was ordained. There was obviously no lack of priests. But the clergy did not just consist of priests. Lower orders (acolytes, lecturers, deacons) were frequent and popular, sometimes only because they were useful, such as for a career in a public position or in science. Membership of an order was also bound to ordination. The huge number of people wanting to take holy orders was to a large extent not merely a result of a religious need to do so: In monasteries and convents there was a certain amount of movement ensuring both economic security and a certain degree of independence from the narrow regulations laid down by urban society. For women, especially from noble families, a nunnery was often the only way to escape from an existence as a submissive and meticulously monitored wife. Then there was the fact that convents were also privileged places of education, so that the convent was almost the only path to a scholarly career. There was an astonishingly wide variety of different types of priests, ranging from the priest for the simple people, who looked after a church belonging to a feudal overlord and could just about recite mass in Latin, the canon at a collegiate church in town who – if he did not live in a collegiate community as was originally expected – dwelt with his servants in a large urban house and had virtually no pastoral duties, to the princely archbishop of noble stock who had so many other tasks that he only very occasionally found the time for his spiritual office. Celibacy was not taken too seriously in the Middle Ages. The majority of priests lived with a woman, and this was even officially allowed in return for a small fee paid to the bishop, although the pope often issued warnings on the matter.

Training for the clergy was usually in the form of a kind of apprenticeship with the local priest, who also selected the candidates. Only larger towns could afford cathedral schools with proper training. One particular bone of contention in the Middle Ages was the prebend system. A prebend was understood to be a spiritual office if it could lay claim to tithes from believers. The tithes, i.e. the tenth of one's revenue to be paid to the church plus fees for christenings, marriages, burials, etc., formed the basis of the priest's livelihood. As a rule, these tithes had four uses: Part went to the parish priest, part to the bishop, part was for church buildings and part for the church's poor, i.e. monasteries and scholars at the schools. There were, however, certain subtle differences between rich prebends, which received valuable tithes, and poor prebends. It was on these distinctions that the clergy concentrated their attention in the Middle Ages. And this was the cause of all the endless complaints about the avarice and corruption of the clergy that abound in the literature of the day. In 1219, Pope Honorius III noted in his study of the effects of the 1215 reform council: "The servants of the altar are like cattle, but they not only moulder in their own excrement but even brag about their sins before Sodom and make no secret of them; they are debased, a snare for the people." Saint Hildegard of Bingen calls the prelates "true robbers of the Church; in their avarice they devour everything they can get their hands on." There was indeed tremendous abuse. High noblemen used their good relations with Rome to get distant episcopal prebends without having the intention of ever setting foot in them. The obligation laid on bishops – or a deputy – to be resident in their sees for at least a few days each year is testimony of this state of affairs. Temporal and spiritual dignitaries transferred important prebends to their relatives even if these were unsuited for the task or had not even been ordained. Seven-year-old boys became clerics and owners of prebends, and it was not until Pope Alexander III (1159–1181) was in office that the minimum age of holding a prebend was set at 14(!). Mediaeval church books are full of accounts of disputes between bishops, monasteries, deans and priests on the right to receive tithes, usufruct and benefices. Documents were forged. It was possible to sell or trade everything. "We sell Christ more shamefully than Judas, but we are worse than he because he thought Christ was a mere man, but we know He is the true God and Man and we still sell Him. He sold Christ for thirty pieces of silver, but we do it for a dinar and the lowest possible wage" (Petrus Cantor, deacon at Reims cathedral, 1130–1197).

Saint Michael (book miniature, c. 1450)
Angels and saints were the permanent and invisible companions of human beings during their earthly existence. They defended Christians from the dangers of everyday life, protected them from the temptations of the devil; they also often gave sinners their due punishment. This picture shows St. Michael struggling with Lucifer, who is lying defeated on the ground with a cross-staff in his throat.

3. Piety, Hagiolatry, Superstition

What was it that bound the people of those days to the Church – a Church that certainly did not present itself without "spot, or wrinkle" (Ephesians 5:27)? Can we look into the hearts, into the piety of mediaeval Christians? There might well be some clues in the following lines written by a monk called Ruotger at the beginning of an account of the life of Archbishop Bruno of Cologne (953–965): "It is true wisdom to know where the gifts one has come from, so that one does not think one has them from oneself (...) If we ask what is our due, we find nothing but punishment. God's mercy came upon us with His grace, (...) because God wanted it, not because Man has deserved it." This is not mere theology. The blunt comparison of the unworthiness of Man and deserved divine grace was probably part of the temper of the Middle Ages. The powerlessness of Man in the face of the powers of nature, disease and death were felt much more intensely than nowadays, likewise the bottomless pit of human wickedness, the appalling effects of sin. The gift of life itself, every moment granted, salvation from incurable disease and finally the mercy of heaven towards sinners must have seemed like the pure grace of the almighty, omnipresent God. This extremely pessimistic and yet religious attitude gave rise to two forms of piety: hagiolatry, i.e. worship of the saints, of those who have already come to God and can intercede on behalf of Man, and an intensive relationship with, even a great longing for that which comes after the vale of tears on this earth, for life after death. Thus Ruotger closes his life of Bruno with the sentence, "He was carried off from this sullied earth and rests in the Lord."

But not everyone could expect to rest in the Lord like the worthy archbishop. Many people had good reason to fear punishment in Hell, which was a focal point of the mediaeval imagination. There is a verse summing up what awaits sinners in Hell: "Pix, nix, nox, – vermis, flagra, vincula, – pus, pudor, horror" (pitch, snow, night, the worm, the scourge, fetters, pus, shame, horror). According to the visions and legends of the day, the punishments of Hell befitted the individual misdemeanors of the damned: Thus a nun who had had an abortion had to carry a burning child; a man who had wrongfully taken possession of ploughland had to carry the burden of the ploughland on his shoulders. To top it all, the devils who prepared such terrors were also present on earth and had to be feared at all times. They would be looking over the monks' shoulders, counting the syllables slurred over during prayer; they would wander through monastery dormitories at night; they hid away in the cavities of the body; they spoke with the voices of the mad. People knew exactly where they stood when the devils appeared with monkey faces and buckhorns, as dogs, ravens and blacks, or as seductive women and beautiful youths. It didn't always help to throw the ink pot at them. Only fervent prayer, going to mass, alms-giving and various magic rites could give help for a while. The invocation of the saints was particularly important. Angels and saints were constant and invisible companions in the life of the people; they protected them from the temptations of the devil, but they often also executed on earth the punishment due to sinners (such as the angel of the Lord who in 871 stripped bishop Gunther of Xanten of his holy vestments in front of the altar and killed him because he had wanted to celebrate mass in spite of having been excommunicated). On the Day of Judgement, which was expected to come at the end of time and which no one would be able to escape, sinners would be able to place all their hopes on the intercession of the saints with a stern but just God. This was why Mary in particular, the eternally virginal and merciful Mother of God, filled hearts with more love and trust than God himself, who was fatherly but stern.

Mary, the Keeper of the World and Comforter of the Distressed, headed the list of saints who, partly through their intervention on earth, partly through their intercession in heaven, influenced life here. The most important saints owed their reputation less to their holiness on earth than to the number of miracles they performed after death. Churches and children were named after them to increase the chances of receiving their protection and support. The bones of the saints were reputed to have a greater influence. A newly discovered shrine of a saint was a public sensation, as was the bringing of relics bought elsewhere to one's own church, such as when in 1164 the bones of the Three Kings were solemnly received in Cologne. It was strictly forbidden by Rome to take the relics of the saints apart, but this was nevertheless a common occurrence in the land of the Franks. There were no bounds to the activities of ingenious profiteers. Goldsmiths devoted their art to making reliquaries, and were paid for doing so. Money and wares were laid as offerings at the altars of the saints; some people rundertook to pay for the expensive candles at the altar. There were several saints who did particularly well and shone in the glory of innumerable miracles until

The Black Prayer Book (15th century)
The genre known as the book of hours belongs to the best of medieval manuscript painting. The book of hours was initially only intended for princes, but after about 1400 it began to be used by rich patricians wishing to own a devotional book similar to the breviary of clerics. The "Black Prayer Book" from Belgium shown here is a particularly beautiful example of this genre. Its name comes from the black parchment used. The miniature shows a scene from the Passion of Christ: the Saviour before Pontius Pilate.

ILL PAGE 98:
God the Father as an architect (Bible moralisée, mid-13th century)
The architects of the great cathedrals saw their task as imitating the divine act of creation. They imagined the creation of the world as being like the process of architectural construction: God the Father, with a compass in his right hand and pushing the globe along in front of him, is ordering the world according to "measure and number and weight" (Wisdom of Solomon, 11:21)

ILL. PAGE 99:
Bible moralisée (mid-13th century)
The Bible was an inexhaustible source for medieval manuscript painting. The book miniaturist was able to refer to various illustration layouts. One of the most interesting is without doubt the "Bible moralisée." On each page of this type of book, there are four biblical scenes depicted on the left in roundels, which are typologically, morally and allegorically interpreted on the right.

The shrine of the Three Kings (1181 c. 1230, Cologne cathedral)

The shrine of the Three Kings, also known as the "Golden Shrine," is regarded as the greatest, most artistic and most valuable reliquary of the Middle Ages. It was made by Nicholas of Verdun, one of the most famous of medieval artists, to hold the mortal remains of the Three Kings – brought to Cologne in about 1164. The reliquary is in the shape of a basilica with a nave and two aisles and seven bays, and is remarkable for its extremely splendid and lavish decor of enamel work, filigree and precious stones.

Imperial crown (10th century)

The crown, made for Otto the Great between 953 and 962, is an impressive testimony of the work of medieval goldsmiths. It is also important because of its symbolism. The cross and the arch were added in the 11th century. The crown is a sign of imperial rule and for contemporaries was a symbol for the Holy Roman Empire. Once, at a time of political confusion, Walther von der Vogelweide called upon the Staufer Philipp of Swabia to put on the crown.

ILL. PAGE 101:

Emperor Henry the Saint (c. 1260, detail of window in Strasbourg cathedral)
Stained glass windows were an important aspect of medieval art. The windows depicted biblical scenes, the lives of saints and founder figures. The magnificent, coloured windows gave church and cathedral walls an illuminated look. The Cistercian monks put plain, colourless windows in their churches – in conscious contrast to the pomp of ecclesiastical buildings in towns.

The northern rose-window in Notre Dame in Paris
(built 1134–1194)
The rose-windows in French cathedrals are a particularly eloquent proof of the excellence of medieval stained glass. Here, this art reached a remarkable peak. A round window can have various symbolic meanings – as the sun it can represent Christ, as a rose the Virgin Mary. Pictures of the redeemer and the Mother of God are placed in the centre of the window. A rose-window can sometimes depict the heavenly Jerusalem, the city of God, which was occasionally imagined to be round.

they, too, stopped being talked about. The fame and reputation of a town very much depended on the number of relics within its walls – a point of view that is of little importance nowadays. *Tempora mutantur.*

Times have perhaps changed a little less in terms of the survival of pre-Christian paganism, which continued into the Middle Ages (and is partly being revived today). The old Germanic gods might have been toppled from power, but no one knew for sure whether some of the demons and spirits, gnomes and forest beings might not still be a menace or an aid. To be on the safe side, it was advisable to put lights and gifts at certain springs, trees and rocks. A closer look at some of the Christian customs of those days reveals them to be a continuation of pagan rites. Some of the saints, such as the virgins Fides (Faith), Spes (Hope), and Caritas (Charity), who were revered in the Eifel region, were possibly nothing more than pre-Christian gods under the guise of a new name. If we consider Gothic cathedrals with their enigmatic gnomes, gargoyles and demons we discover one of the ways the Middle Ages reconciled paganism and Christianty: "Ecclesia benedicat omnia" (The Church blesses everything) – and in doing so makes it its own.

The murder of the boy Simon in Trent (woodcut, 1493)
Ritual murders of Christians, supposed to have been committed by Jews, were an excuse for pogroms against the Jews. In 1294, it was rumoured that in Zaragoza in Spain Jews had cruelly and brutally slaughtered a Christian boy. The matter was brought to court, where it was discovered that the accusation against the Jewish community was merely based on lies.

4. The Outsiders of Christendom: Jews and Heretics

We have already spoken of mediaeval society as being "Christendom." In the 11th century, at the latest, with the investitures controversy and the beginning of Church reform, it started seeing itself more and more clearly in this light. In spite of all the differences between villages, towns and regions, the Middle Ages made sure of its unity by clinging to the same faith, Church, rites and customs. It is also in the 11th century that we first come across violence against the Jewish community, and first see larger-scale heretical movements taking hold of the population. Every organized entity, including Christendom, has its outsiders. The way Christians treated those who threatened their unity is, no matter what other base motives there might have been, typical of regular attempts in the course of history to use force to achieve uniformity. Catholicism or proscription, persecution, death – these were the alternatives in the Middle Ages for people wanting to escape from the only true system of spiritual and temporal power.

There had always been Jews living in the West. They dwelt in special quarters in the towns and differed from Christians in their dress, language and church services. But the Holy Scripture they shared with Christians (the Old Testament) and the strictly patriarchal order within the family and community showed there were also some similarities. There were no problems when it came to Jews and Christians doing business with each other, especially since Christians were not allowed to charge each other interest, while Jews were allowed to do so with non-believers. Bishops and kings often approached Jewish merchants when they were short of money. During periods of persecution, Jews were very often able to buy special rights of protection from those in power. There were international contacts within the Jewish community, and so the Jews were particularly easily available for long-distance trading. It was not long before they had "Christian" competition in this field, a result of economic progress during the 12th century. If we bear in mind the large debts many Christians owed to Jewish moneylenders, the pogroms against the Jews – the first big wave took place at the beginning

The Coronation of the Virgin Mary (mid-13th century)
Not only the huge number of poems about the Virgin Mary bear witness to the reverence paid to the Mother of God, but also the many representations in the fine arts. The Virgin Mary, the "rose without thorns," the "keeper of the world" and "comforter of the distressed" was regarded as the most important of the saints; it was she to whom people turned in times of need and who it was hoped would intercede with the Heavenly Father.

of the first crusade (1096) – appear to be more than just an expression of misguided religious fanaticism. Various factors would have incited the progroms. It was about this time that the first stories of atrocities committed by the Jews started circulating, as in 1294 in Zaragoza in Spain, where they were said to have kidnapped a Christian boy, beheaded him and removed his liver and heart to make a devilish brew. There were court proceedings, the charge turned out to be untrue and the boy was discovered in the charge of a Christian slave trader. What remained, however, were deep-seated prejudices against the Jews in the town, their public proscription and discrimination. The Jews were always "the others"; they were always different from the Christians; in the end, however, it was not the former who changed, but the latter, and the Jews had to foot the bloody bill. Public disputations held in many towns between Christian and Jewish theologians only superficially followed the path of reason. It was clear from the beginning how these disputations would end; if the Jews taking part were not prepared to recognize that the man crucified on the cross was the true God, that He had a right to alter Mosaic Law and that He redeemed the world, they were just confirming their reputation as stubborn, hard-hearted people. It was then a matter for the Christian ruler to decide whether they should be let off in grace or sentenced to death. The custom in Toulouse of getting the bishop to box the ears of the leader of the Jewish community after every Easter mass was, by comparison, mild. If a Jew, like young Judas from Cologne (c. 1125), voluntarily converted to Christianity, it was not because he felt he had been disproved by the arguments of the theologians. Rather, he was impressed by the human gesture of the episcopal supervisor in Münster who, during a meal with the bishop, gave him, an ostracized Jew, half a bread roll and a helping of salmon while he himself made do with bread and water. The convert Judas, who gave himself the Christian name Hermann, had to bear the full brunt of the coldness and disapproval of his one-time brothers in faith.

The Christian Middle Ages were also a time of the wildest Christian heresies. There were Cathari and Waldenses, Publicans and Patarines, Albigenses and Petrobrusians and Arnoldists and many others, although some of the names stood for one and the same group. They all undertook to question the truth and legitimacy of the Catholic Church. When we talk of heretics today, we often mean people representing certain liberal views compared to the strict dogmas of the Church (or a political party, etc.). The term had very different connotations in the Middle Ages. Almost all mediaeval heretical sects came to the conclusion that the Catholic Church was not severe enough, not rigorous enough and, above all, not in accordance with the simple spirit of Christ – and that it was therefore to be rejected. There is a good deal to be said for the theory that the heretic communities were really a Church reform movement that did not manage to remain within the Church. This is why they sometimes seem to be exactly the same as those reform groups, such as the movement of begging monks, that stayed in the Church. Poverty, rejection of wordly power, and a life like that led by Jesus and His apostles were what they all had in common. In any case, the fact that from the 12th century onwards there were heretic sects attracting large sections of the population shows clearly how deep-seated Christianity already was, since a certain degree of independence of thought and religious beliefs is necessary if emancipation from Church leadership is to be possible.

Let us first take a look at the most important of the mediaeval heretical sects, the Cathari. The word comes from Greek and means "the pure ones." A monk called Cäsarius of Heisterbach, who could well be called the court reporter of the day, describes one of their meetings in a cellar, "to which many people of both sexes came. The leader gave a sermon full of blasphemies, after which the light was extinguished and each person mingled with the flesh of the person nearest to him, without distinguishing between wife and unmarried girl, between widow and virgin, between mistress and maid, between sister and daughter." The imagination of the devout Cäsarius seems to have run away with him, and with propagandist aims into the bargain. In reality, the Catharists, the pure ones, were severe in their rejection of sexual intercourse as sin and expected their leaders, the "perfecti" (the perfect ones), to refrain entirely from it. They even went as far as to forbid the consumption of everything resulting from copulation (meat, milk, cheese, eggs, etc., with the exception of fish). But this was a demand kept only by the "perfecti," who called themselves apostles; their followers (audientes) were guided in their actions by the leaders without, however, always doing exactly as they did. The Cathari had a highly pessimistic and dualistic view of life: there are two principles – an evil one (materialistic) and a good one (spiritual) – fighting each other, but during life on earth the evil principle gains the upper hand because the world has been created by an evil demiurge (whom they equate with the Old Testament god Yahweh). Salvation is only possible by discarding, on this earth, all that is material and of the flesh, all cravings and desires. More objective reports about the Cathari just say that they led a simple, continent and

Queribus rock fortress
The Cathari were the most powerful and important of the heretical sects in the 12th and 13th centuries. They rejected sexual intercourse as a sin, avoided all products originating from copulation (meat, milk, eggs, etc.) and were highly critical of what they regarded as the lax attitude of the Church towards sinners. The Cathari were particularly popular in southern France and northern Italy. The Inquisition used harsh punishments in an attempt to stamp out these heresies. Our picture shows the fortress of Queribus in the Pyrenees, the highest place of refuge of the Cathari.

The Marienburg (c. 1280–end of the 14th century) During the Crusades, orders of knights were established – religious communities whose members took monastic vows and did chivalrous war service to defend and spread the faith. The oldest of these orders was the Order of the Hospital of Saint John of Jerusalem, founded in 1110 in Jerusalem and which, like the Knights Templar (est. 1119) or the Brethren of the Sword (est. 1202), made it their task to fight "infidels" and devote themselves to the care of the sick. Our picture shows the Marienburg on the River Nogat, which after 1309 was the seat of the Grand Master of the Teutonic Order of Knights. The Teutonic Order was established in 1198. It swallowed up the Order of the Brethren of the Sword in 1237, and this, together with its expansive power politics in the Baltic region, allowed it to develop into a tremendously important order.

honest life. They rejected the Catholic Church, with its involvement in matters of this world, its enjoyment of sensual pleasures and its laxity towards sinners. There was no justification for ecclesiastical offices, and neither for any of the sacraments; they thought Jesus Christ was an angel and not the Son of God. This was a challenge to the Church. The church response began with theological arguments and diatribes such as those written by Cäsarius, but in the end violent repression seemed the only form of salvation. The Third Lateran Council (1179) passed the following resolution: "We enjoin all believers manfully to resist these epidemics and to protect with weapons all Christian people. The goods and property of the heretics are to be confiscated, and the princes may subject such people to slavery." Princes, together with spiritual authorities, made good use of this liberty – after all, it was not just a matter of executing people but also of seizing their property – because they, too, saw heresies as an attack on the unity of their people. In the early days, however, the persecution of the heretics turned out to be a difficult business. Representatives of the Church sent to investigate this problem regularly discovered that people suspected of being heretics claimed to be Catholics if they were asked about their religious faith, but no sooner had the Church commission turned its back than they returned to their old heresies. This led to the formation of the Inquisition (meaning "enquiry," "investigation") so that suitable ways could be used of finding out who really was a heretic. A "very thorough interrogation," i.e. interrogation under torture, became the rule; in his "Manual of Inquisitorial Practice" (c. 1323) Bernhard Gui, a Dominican bishop in southern France and the most prominent of the inquisitors in the Middle Ages, devotes quite a degree of misanthropic perspicacity to methods of establishing true heresies. The Cathari sect, who dominated large parts of southern France and northern Italy in the 12th and 13th centuries, were liquidated with great intolerance, bloodshed and cruelty. The Cathari were barely able to gain a foothold in Germany. The only Cathari trial in Germany was in 1143 in Cologne and ended with three death sentences.

The strictly dualistic concept of the Cathari religious beliefs (the idea of there being an evil and a good principle), as well as names like Bulgarians, Manichaeans, Bogomils used to describe them, is an indication of their non-Christian, Eastern and ancient origins. And indeed, the dualistic explanation of evil in the world is a legacy of certain philosophies of the late ancient, particularly Persian (Zarathustra) worlds and of gnostic concepts. Even today, this concept still has its supporters because of its extreme simplicity. The Cathari movement in the Middle Ages effectively revived it. But on the other hand there were other sects of heretics trying to combat Catholic Christendom simply with the spirit of the gospel. The Waldenses were the most important of these sects. Their founder, a merchant by the name of Peter Waldo from Lyon, saw a stark contrast between the wealth of the Church and the poverty of the apostles as depicted in the Bible. He gave away everything he owned to the poor and in simple clothes – in very much the same way as St. Francis – began the life of an itinerant and penitential preacher. Because he and his followers only ever wore wooden shoes called sabots, they were also called "Sabbatati." Waldo attended the Council in 1179 and tried to get the Church to recognise his sect – a recognition he was given on condition that he and his people would preach on behalf of the Church. The Waldenses did not keep to this agreement for long. Their lay preachers started turning up in villages and towns where they preached the pure gospel, declared mass held by unworthy (e.g. married) priests to be invalid and pilloried the wealth of the Church. They rejected the concept of purgatory, prayers for the dead and the requiem mass, adoration of the saints, indulgences, oaths, military service and the death penalty; the only sacraments they recognized were baptism, Holy Communion and penance (as did Martin Luther and the Reformation later on). This led to their excommunication. They, too, were to become victims of the Inquisition. At the Synod of Verona (1184) Pope Lucius III and Frederick Barbarossa together declared the decree of excommunication against heretics, their followers and defenders, placed them under the ban of the Empire and ordered that the bishops search for heretics once or twice a year in suspicious places and that temporal authorities punish the guilty according to their instructions. The Waldenses partly survived the persecution. In 1532, Waldenses in France joined the Calvinists. Even today, there are still some 45,000 Waldenses in Italy.

Execution by the wheel and boiling in oil (from the Spiez Chronicles, 1485)
The Middle Ages were extremely inventive and cruel when it came to punishing misdeeds. In an age of superstition, not only men and women were burned as heretics and witches; animals were also victims of the judiciary. The "Sachsenspiegel," for example, called for animals to be killed for "refusing to give help" if they were found near the scene of a crime to human beings.

The Fine Arts in the High Middle Ages
by Peter Gerlach

Pulley and wooden ladder (from Bible dating from the beginning of the 13th century)
Wooden ladders have been used from time immemorial to carry building materials up onto a higher level. Pulleys were used to pull up mortar in tubs and buckets and small stones. In the picture above (behind the pulley) we can see a plumb level being used to monitor the upper edge of the wall.

Stonemason's yard (c. 1220/30)
Stonemasons were not only in charge of manufacturing ashlars; they were also responsible for making columns, capitals, and reliefs. Our picture gives the reader a view of a stonemason's yard and shows two stages in the manufacture of a stone sculpture. The stonemason's tools – wooden mallet and chisel – can be clearly seen on the right.

Outstanding achievements in all three branches of the fine arts, i.e. painting (panel painting and book illuminations), carving (sculpture and goldsmithery) and architecture (building cathedrals and towns and secular architecture), are characteristic of the high Middle Ages. Each branch has its own special characteristics, yet they are all united by the same tendencies that distinguish art of this period from art of earlier epochs. The turning point was in the 11th–12th centuries, but it was not so much a break as a change in style connected with changing ideas and concepts and can already be seen in the earliest work of this period. The way art then developed lay in the way this new beginning grew and evolved. It is significant that this epoch ended when cathedral building also came to an end. According to Panofsky, this principle of the domination of one particular style can be understood to be the illustration of metaphysical concepts expressed both in architecture and in the interpretative arts. The factor common to all branches of art in the central period of the Middle Ages is a symbolic presentation of the Christian view of the world; and in the process, nature and the historic present were increasingly included in this typological form.

The end of the Middle Ages is not marked by a rediscovery of the classical world – which is present in various ways in every stage of the Middle Ages; rather, it is linked with a departure from tradition and, at different times in different regions, a turning towards a changed view of the world. There is no logical reason for this development, neither can it be traced back to the way art had hitherto been developing. If the history of ideas in the Middle Ages can be said to be centred on scholarship, the works of the fine arts – the towns and universities as social forms of organization and the cathedrals as centres of religious practice – contributed specifically to the development of these new forms. Together they all formed a mutual style as constituent elements.

Contrary to what might be expected, the main drive behind the creation of new works of art was not the land-developing monasteries and their considerable artistic achievements, but urban centres, where important works of sacral art were created. Certainly, some secular princely and urban-bourgeois buildings from this period have survived, and there are plenty of buildings connected with transport, such as bridges and town gates. And yet it is those large churches built in cathedral towns that are *the* buildings that continue to be associated with this entire period. There are a number of reasons for this. Firstly, social groups, each with their own individual interests, were involved in the building process. Secondly, these huge projects led to the establishment of new technologies and forms of business organization. Before building could begin, the financing had to be arranged, and this involved both the bishop as the territorial overlord and other groups, who were now also able to be bring their own interests to bear. The fact that these people saw themselves as represented by public buildings meant that these buildings became centres of urban social life. Artisans learned very specialized crafts and thus became available long-term for such projects, and the necessary materials had to be obtained – all this not only took advantage of traditional feudal services, but also made necessary new forms of financing for such projects and the use of means of transport hitherto not locally available. The financial situation was improved by the increase in long-distance trade and the beginnings of publishing, while the experiences of precisely this new economic form were useful for the transport system.

The bishop and chapter could contribute services from forced labour, and money and income from church collections, penance fines and indulgences; to this were added donations from local guilds and urban fraternities making essential contributions to the financing of the building and its fittings. Materials were standardized and this meant that building techniques were rationalised. Preliminary work could now be done in the mason's yard during the winter months. Work during the rest of the year was not only made easier but also considerably speeded up by the introduction of new lifting mechanisms. The architect, who is usually unnamed, generally came from the laity. As the person in charge of such a complicated and progressive organization, he rose from the status of an artisan to join the privileged rank of master masons and master builders, who became designing and organizing architects. We can, with a certain degree of certainty, say that they used plans drawn to scale to help them in their work. Indeed, such scale plans could well be their invention, since they are not known to have existed in earlier periods. The fact that these early architects were able to design several highly individual buildings, either simultaneously or in quick succes-

Saint Denis (ambulatory, built between 1141 and 1144)
Abbot Suger of St. Denis (1081–1151) was responsible for the building plans for the abbey church of St. Denis. He was not only the regent of France between 1147 and 1149, but also made a name for himself as a writer. In the ambulatory shown here, we can see two features of design typical of Gothic architecture. Firstly, the aim was to reduce the masonry to make room for big windows; and secondly, a large number of columns were erected to increase the tectonic stability.

Three examples of Gothic circular windows
The stone filigree in the windows – the tracery –
acted as a framework to hold the ever larger windows together, especially in the late Gothic period.
Top: Romanesque wheel window with simple
ornamentation (San Rufino, Assisi, Italy)
Centre: Rose-window in Lincoln (England); so-
called "curvilinear style"
Bottom: Rose-window in Chartres (France)

sion and making use of the same technical principles, is an indication of their organizational and technical skill.

All the creative elements used by Gothic architects can be seen as early as the 12th century in the ambulatory of the choir in the abbey church of St. Denis (1141–1144). The following can be mentioned: firstly, the walls have become thinner, making possible large windows providing scope for the glazier with his stained glass paintings; secondly, tectonic stability is provided by clustered columns, the form of which shows they are intended to support the arches. In the lower part, these columns are also a many-layered frame for the transparent glass windows and, in the upper part, for the colourfully painted sections of the arches.

The idea of the diaphanous wall applies here. Accordingly, Gothic cathedral architecture is seen as a picture. The frame itself is in turn a representation of "rational" architectural elements. The slender engaged columns surrounding the solid piers have no real bearing function, but they do form a three-dimensionally filigree system of interlacing, in the spaces of which the rest of the walls remain spread out "as thin as paper" (Vasari). It must therefore seem to be a logical continuation if, in the cathedrals built immediately after St. Denis (Sens 1140–1168, Noyon 1174–1200, Laon 1190–1195), the opening wall is split into two shells by galleries and triforia, the outer, rear one now also appears to be shining as a result of the outside light. Finally, the rosette in the west wall increases in size (Amiens 1220/1230, Saint-Denis 1231/1245, Reims 1250/1300), and this makes the outer wall, too, in this part of the building into a subtle structure of stained glass painting and picture frame. The climax of this presentation of the inside of a church, with its mystical symbolism of light, must surely be Sainte-Chapelle in Paris (c. 1243–48), the colouring of which is a particularly good illustration of the transparency of the outside surface of the enclosed space.

The rational calculations uniting function and design in one splendidly self-contained work of art can be seen more clearly on the exterior of Gothic cathedrals than inside. The number of side chapels intended to hold tombs and with an altar of their own was forever being increased and this meant that more and more adjunct spaces had to be added, particularly to the choir, ambulatory and, finally, the nave as well. By the time Notre Dame in Paris (c. 1245–c. 1300/1330) and St. Julien in Le Mans (consecrated 1254) were built, Gothic architects had been able to slim down the flying buttresses and supporting pillars from the stocky forms and solid pillars used at Reims (1194–1220?) into an architecture as delicate outside as the architectural forms inside were light and dainty. It is not until all possibilities, such as pointed arches, outside buttresses, ribbed vaulting – all forms which can individually be found in previous buildings – were systematically used together to form a constructive unity that Gothic architects felt able to use them in their many and increasingly daring variations. It is, therefore, hardly possible to speak of linear development. In general terms, the development fell into four phases.

The first phase (1140–1190) was dominated by the cathedral as the main form of ecclesiastical building in the Île de France. At this time, late Romanesque churches were still being built in Germany and Italy which, in their external form but not as far as the thinking behind the construction were concerned, can be compared with Gothic architecture. The expansion of this new Gothic building took place in a second phase

Cologne cathedral
The building of the great cathedrals of France
started as early as the mid-12th century, at a time
when ecclesiastical architecture in Germany was
still very much dominated by the Romanesque
style. It was not until 1235, when work started on
St. Elizabeth's in Marburg, that Gothic architecture
also began to become established in Germany.
Cologne cathedral was commenced in 1248
(though not completed till the 19th century) and is
regarded as the first German cathedral to be
entirely built in Gothic style.

(1190–1250) as French Crown lands were being added to. At the same
time as this was happening, there were special forms (Early English,
c. 1175–1250) being built in Normandy and England, which developed
independently and occasionally influenced buildings in France. It was
not until 1220 that the Gothic style of French cathedrals found its way to
Western Spain. Gothic, as an architectural style for cathedrals, is not
found all over Europe until phase three (1250–1300), although even then
a modified form of Gothic adapted to more modest needs and local
possibilities developed. This local form, found specifically in Germany
and in England (Decorated style, c. 1250–1340; Perpendicular from 1340),
shares with the cathedral style only certain principles of structure. In
Germany, the Romanesque tradition of building remained alive until
the middle of the 13th century. It was not until Cologne cathedral was
started in 1248 that French cathedral architecture asserted itself – after
work on St. Elizabeth's in Marburg had already been commenced in
1235, which had been designed as a homogenous whole along the lines
of Early Gothic cathedrals like that in Laon in northern France.

    If the pointed arch is the characteristic feature of the interior, then
outside it is the buttresses. Both dominate the outward appearance of

Dwelling tower in Regensburg (13th century)
There was a huge growth in the urban population in the 13th century, and this caused a number of architectural problems. Space in towns was limited by the town wall and thus there was virtually no scope for expansion, meaning that architects and builders were forced to build upwards. This gave towns a distinctive visual character – narrow, crooked alleys and houses with extensions and additional storeys added at a later date were typical features. The above picture shows an early example of medieval urban architecture.

this style; both were means used by mediaeval architects to design ever new variations of their daring constructions. These designs were binding for the building process, but only a few of them are extant. The pointed arch made it possible to join parts of the interior of varying widths together under one canopy. In contrast to the square ground-plan system of the Romanesque style, the broader spans of the central nave, the narrower bays of the side aisles (of which there were up to three), the trapeziform bays of the ambulatory and the semicircular bays of the chapels are all constructed according to one common pattern because the bend at the highest point of the arch allows it to be spread out at varying degrees. The buttresses and flying buttresses helped carry the weight of the supporting masonry, thus allowing the cathedrals to be built to considerable heights. Finally, by using tracery, the interior walls – after the introduction of the triforia – could almost totally be broken up. Tracery and buttresses, which, particularly when Gothic was at its height, become highly complicated art forms, now completely cover up their architectural importance. It was not until late Gothic that the ribbed vaults were given an increasingly complicated structure (fan vaulting, hammer vaulting, etc.) until it finally became a decorative feature independent of the construction, although it still had the function of "depicting" the vault of the sky.

The moulding of the supporting parts of the building by the responds is matched in the open, rising walls to the stone tracery with which the tall slender windows were structured. First the trefoil and then later the many-foiled tracery are the main forms and are arranged either radially or axially. In the late phase, the Perpendicular and French Flamboyant styles (developed in England after 1350 and found all over the continent after 1370) became lace-like in their tracery.

Not only cathedral architecture is important. The more austere and less ornate architecture of churches and monasteries also had a significant role to play. The building regulations of the Cistercian and mendicant monks can be seen as critique of the urban cathedral buildings, of the effort and expense invested in their construction, in their extravagant decoration and wealthy adornment. Thus, the Cistercians had no stone belfry, and their glazed windows were without colour and images. All kinds of images and sculptures were banned from inside their churches, since they were claimed to distract from proper meditation and interfere with the necessary religious earnestness. The mendicant orders began to build their own simple churches later than the Cistercians. Even if there was no ground-plan common to these churches, it is nevertheless possible to point to a number of salient features they had in common.

There was on principle no transept; the most popular type of building was the hall church, i.e. a church with a nave and aisles of the same height, or a flat-roofed hall, sometimes a flat-roofed basilica. The choir also generally had a flat roof. The dominant feature of the exterior is carefully fitted masonry of great precision, and in spite of its lack of ornamentation the interior presents an impressive picture with its painted stones. Monastery buildings, chapter houses, dormitories and refectories are more richly decorated. Similarities between these buildings and urban secular architecture are more likely than between cathedrals and secular buildings. The town and guild halls, cloth halls and staple-houses are a permanent expression of the wealth and independence of town citizens. There are luxuriously furnished public buildings that have survived, particularly in the town republics of Upper Italy, in the free imperial towns in Germany and in Flanders, even though extensive restoration and rebuilding have been necessary.

Pictures and sculptures were dominated by the concept of typology – the symbolic and exemplary character of Old Testament figures, objects and events for New Testament and historic persons and their deeds – as a visualization of events connected with Christian salvation. This is true of the great didactic tympanum reliefs in cathedrals with their representations of the Day of Judgement. It is also true, towards the end of the period in question, of illustrations in books for private prayer and meditation, in which living persons (founders and commissioners of ecclesiastical buildings) document their *imitatio pietatis* by having their own faces added to pictures of the saints.

It is an open question to what extent the appearance of the portraits of artists in a sacral context can be understood to be typological concepts extended into the historical present. In any case, the prominent importance of the depiction of people presupposes Gothic sculpture, particularly cathedral and funerary sculpture. Although the figures of a bishop and a king in a portrayal of the Virgin Mary in the tympanum of the right-hand western portal on Notre Dame in Paris (1150/60) cannot with any certainty be said to represent historical figures, it is nevertheless clear that these sculptures, in spite of the fact that they are part of a relief, are the beginning of free sculpture portraits, an art that was soon after to peak in Chartres. The individualization of movements and physiognomy in Reims and Strasbourg (south portal, c. 1235) pointed the way to the naturalism of the 14th century in particular, of which a typical example is the bust of Peter Parlér (c. 1380) in the cathedral of St. Vitus in Prague. A comparable conquest of the illusionary free space is to be found in the mural paintings in the papal court in Avignon, or in Italian towns – in paintings by Simone Martini, Duccio and Giotto, or, taking us now to the realm of landscape painting, in the wall decorations of 1337–39 by Ambrogio Lorenzetti in the Sala della Pace of the Palazzo Pubblico, Siena. In Italian sculpture, Nicolo Pisano, with his human figures largely detached from the background of the relief, not only achieved something comparable to French cathedral sculpture; with his work, modelled on classical sculpture, he also went further than the achievements in northern Europe.

The scenes depicted in Bamberg, Mainz and Naumburg (c. 1250) are marked by the individuality of the faces. Typically, the figures of the long-dead church founders have been brought up to date in the clothes of the 13th century. But this is not the case with Christ, Madonnas and saints; here specific types were developed and these were adhered to over a long period of time. The various forms of "devotional pictures" also belong here – crucifix of branches with the martyred body of Christ, pietà, Trinity, Virgin of the Protecting Coat, and the special form of the Christ-John group peculiar to southern Germany – they all bear witness to the painful experiences of the people of this period, who saw themselves confronted by the anger of God, who sent famines and epidemics as punishment. Historical experiences, both good and bad, are expressed in works of art.

Compared to Romanesque architecture, the windows were made considerably larger. This gave stained glass, first in French Gothic and then in the rest of Europe, a big chance to develop. But not in Italy, where architecture and, more particularly, painting remained more firmly tied

Saint Stephen (panel painting, mid-13th century) Although in the East wooden panels had long been used as a painting medium (icons), panel painting did not become established in Western art until the end of the 11th century. The earliest pictures painted on wood date back to 1180 and are antependia and retables, i. e. decorated panels for the front and back of the altar. It is not until the second half of the 13th century that panel painting became more widespread, and after that it became a typical aspect of medieval art and painting.

Group with Christ and John (Upper Swabia, c. 1330)
The group belongs to a small number of carvings to be found only in southern Germany, depicting that short passage in the account of the Last Supper according to St. John, which says, "Now there was leaning on Jesus' bosom one of his disciples, whom Jesus loved" (John 13:23). The group with Christ and John is a "devotional picture" which selects a brief moment in the events described in the Bible and depicts it with depth and feeling. The pious beholder can enter into an intensive and emotional relation to Christ by identifying with the scene.

to the continuity of Eastern influence and where, unlike the rest of Europe, there was not a change of style at the beginning of the 12th century.

Although a great many of the old windows have been destroyed, those that have survived can tell us a great deal about the form and contents of stained glass painting. In the same way that Gothic architecture as a whole may be seen as a picture frame, the stained windows contain a programme of instruction for the faithful – the words of the priest were illustrated by glass pictures. These illustrations were an essential component of what has been called the poor man's Bible.

The earliest basic form is the medallion window. In this clearly defined frame, there is a scene from the Bible surrounded by more circles, in which there is room for adjunct figures. Similar patterns to this basic one can be found in the rich illustrations of the "Bible moralisée." And yet square parts of pictures, again comparable to forms of book illustrations, can also be found very early on (St. Denis, before 1145). The remaining spandrels in the medallion windows are filled with ornaments, and the circular patterns themselves extended in many-tiered orders to form quatrefoils or rhombs crossing each other diagonally (Chartres, Notre Dame, c. 1220).

The great achievement as far as the contents are concerned is to be found in the central window of the choir. Here, we usually have a depiction of the Passion of Christ, or of his genealogy, the Tree of Jesse, with relative references to the Old and New Testaments. The northern windows of the nave are the place in which Patriarchs, prophets and patron saints are shown, while opposite them, in the windows to the south, we can find apostles, martyrs and important saints. This compositional and didactic distribution of typological relations is the principle on which God's plan for human salvation makes the church interior into an image of the heavenly Jerusalem and includes the living believer in his earthly world. Logically enough, the actual use of the various parts of the church – for christenings, as a place to hold court proceedings, for the cult of the dead, etc. – was very often taken into account. There are corresponding plans for the arrangement of church sculptures, and these are valid both for inside and out. During this period there are also similar didactic combinations to be found in the illustrations of the new religious books such as "Bible moralisée," "Pictor in carmine," "Speculum humanae salvationis" and "Concordantia caritatis," in altar decorations and frescoes. Even pictures and sculptures in the stately buildings of secular life, like town halls, adhere to this typological principle (prophets' cycle in Cologne, Brussels, Bruges, Bremen, Erfurt and Basle from 1349 onwards).

After about 1225, post-Romanesque art in mural painting and book illumination is characterized by a wealth of stories depicted in great cycles of pictures. Here we find new kinds of pictures that are not bound to older iconographical principles, neither need they be connected in any way to the main scenes. The "Bible moralisée" (post–1226) was commissioned by the royal family in France, as was also the "Liber floridus." Profane texts (chronicles, novels, epic poetry) written in French were illustrated in university circles in Paris (post–1215); the scenes used to decorate the books increasingly incorporated pictorial representations of life as it really was then. The most famous are known as drolleries, i.e. genre figures on the edge of the pages, most of which show lively and descriptive scenes of everyday life, as well as the phan-

tastic and grotesque. The same holds true of the German-language world chronicles, which were illustrated after 1270, mainly in the region around the Upper Rhine and Lake Constance. There are also manuscripts written in central Germany, again in the local vernacular ("Sachsenspiegel" – a compendium of mediaeval law, 1220/1300–1325; "Sächsische Weltchronik" – a history of the world, 1320), and the "Speculum humanae salvationis," which was written in Strasbourg in 1324. All these can be mentioned as examples of pictures with a story to tell, illustrating a form of literature that was rapidly spreading over the whole of Europe. One of the main works is, without doubt, the "Manesse Manuscript" from the region round Lake Constance, which was illustrated in 1313–1330 by three masters.

Regarding style, Gothic art can be divided into three groups, the first of which originated in the Île de France. This group is marked by the soft, elegant flow of the smiling figures, regardless of the situations they are shown to be in. Typical of the High Middle Ages is the concentration of schools of painting around centres – later more particularly urban centres – in which a court or a monastery commissioned works, thus stimulating and concentrating artistic activity, thus giving rise to local schools which had close relations with itinerant artists. Secondly, there were the regional groups developing specific styles. The western, French style, is completely different from the "Zackenstil" of the Thuringian-Saxon school, which probably had its origins in the influence of Byzantine art. The distinctive features of this are the angular lines of the cloth covering the scarcely perceptible anatomy of the figures. Here it is the robe that is the expressive element. These regional forms lost ground, without, however, disappearing entirely, in the face of an increasing standardization that set in after 1300. Very soon afterwards, a style became dominant that had originated in Paris, the centre of French painting, and was marked by elegant, slender figures shrouded in long, flowing robes. This basic soft, flowing style is often called "courtly," but

Klosterneuburg altar (Nicholas of Verdun, detail, consecrated 1181)
Like the shrine of the Three Kings, the Klosterneuburg altar is one of the major pieces of work created by goldsmiths in the 12th century. On each of the wings of the triptych, with its blue and gold enamel, there are three zones, each in a different colour and calling for a precisely defined interpretation on the part of the beholder. The upper (green) zone depicts prefigurations of Christ from the Old Testament ("ante legem"); the middle – reddish – zone shows the Messianic age ("sub gratia"), and the bottom one (bluish) Old Testament scenes of Moses on Mount Sinai ("sub lege"). Our picture is a detail from the middle piece; on the left we can see the birth of Isaac, in the middle Christ's birth and on the right Samson's birth.

Peter Parlér (portrait bust in the cathedral of St. Vitus in Prague, c. 1380)
The Parlérs were the most important family of masons in the 14th century. Peter Parlér's father, Henry, from Cologne, worked as a mason in Gmünd in Swabia. His son was commissioned by Charles IV to build St. Vitus' in Prague, and was responsible for the extensive sculpturing in the Gothic cathedral. His self-portrait shows that during the 14th century it increasingly became the rule for artists to identify themselves.

this does not necessarily mean that it originated in this social milieu. Rather, the term only refers to an appearance of almost elegiac elegance and also touches on the increasingly differentiated facial expressions of the figures.

The background of the paintings, which are generally given an ornamental or architectural frame, remained plain and flat. In the early Middle Ages, the background was usually in gold, but then it started to be filled in with geometrically regular ornamental surfaces, against which the pictorial scenes, with their wealth of overlapping figures, stand out on a thin strip of ground. Depending on the contents and context of the picture, the edge could be either buildings inscribed in the frame or part of the picture.

Apart from Italy and the Franco-Flemish region, it is the Bohemian school, centred on the court of Charles IV in Prague, that spread and was of supraregional importance. The elegance is here replaced by more austere, more solid and increasingly individual figures. Parallel to this, the Italian work of Giotto and Simone Martini was evolving, an art known as "International Gothic" and regarded as being both the climax and the conclusion of the art of the High Middle Ages. Political unrest, the papal schism, and social tension in large parts of Europe are not reflected in the art of the period around 1400. Unlike the beginning of Gothic in the 12th century, however, there was now no dominant centre to stimulate artists. There were various centres from Tuscany to the North Sea coast in close touch with each other, and it was here that pictures and sculptures with common features and similar styles were created. Trade connections were still good, and they brought works of art to all parts of Europe, from England to Bohemia and Austria and right down to Spain. And with the works there came the artists, such as the Parlérs, who travelled from Cologne via Swabia to Prague, or Simone Martini, who went from Siena to Avignon. The invention of the mobile panel painting must now be mentioned because it allowed works apart from book illustrations to be merchandised, works that were of a larger size. And this artistic merchandise, like the works of goldsmiths, spread themes and stylistic innovations. The extensive interrelationship of European royal families was an important contribution to making this art international.

In the early days of Gothic art, gestures were used to indicate that people were associated with each other. Later whole scenes were created, with people involved and talking with each other. This step is marked by an increase in realistic details. In the representation of the history of Christ the Saviour, the central contents were initially limited to a few important characters, their necessary attributes and illustrative gestures. The increase in narrative elements and psychological differentiation by the addition of accompanying figures and scenic backgrounds, which served as a realistic illustration of the situation being depicted, is a sign of a break from traditional pictorial patterns – made possible by a new interest in characteristic details. However, we must not forget that even now a self-contained, Christian view of the world still laid down the details to be used. In the 12th century it still was rare for artists to sign their works (e.g. Antelami on the background of the "Descent from the Cross" in Parma cathedral, 1178; Nicholas of Verdun, Klosterneuburg Altar, 1181, and the Shrine of Our Lady, Turnai, 1205). By the 15th century, however, it had become commonplace. Even so, portraits of artists and church founders (e.g. Peter Parlér in the cathedral

of St. Vitus in Prague, c. 1372) going back to the 14th century must not blind us to the fact that portraits and an increase in facial likeness were reserved for princes, while people of lower rank were allowed to participate in this privilege as subordinates at the most.

The interest in reality and observations of familiar natural surroundings point to another similar field found worthy of portrayal – the beginnings of landscape painting. Very soon afterwards, the limited landscape as the stage for action, such as on French tapestries (The Apocalypse of Angers, 1377, copied from older book illuminations), had both in panel painting and in the illustrations of the books of hours become a rationally preformed cultural landscape to which people dressed in court fashion were added and could be seen doing their daily work – hunting, travelling, ploughing, etc. The composition of the picture is that of an unreal world of the imagination described in the highly developed language of art.

The contents underwent a similar transformation. Iconographic types from the Christian picture tradition could now absorb elements and in doing so develop differing aspects of subjective piety no longer bound to canonical texts or parts of the liturgy. The strict picture parallelism and the early Gothic depiction of figures bound by the outline to the surface became, by the adaptation of classical models, the freely moving, fully moulded and rounded figure of c. 1250. The framed picture, in which dialogic relationships are no longer merely indicated by gestures and are connected to a more comprehensive narrational context by additive accumulation, was now free to evolve – the narrow strip of ground along the bottom of older works now extended upwards and connected human beings naturally with their controlled and structured environment.

Cistercian church in Pontigny (started 1145) Mendicant orders such as the Cistercians built monasteries and churches that were in deliberate contrast to cathedrals. The unadorned churches of the Cistercians are stone testimonies of the ascetic lifestyle of this order. Cistercian masons, for example, ommitted the stone belfry, stained glass windows and pictures and sculptures to decorate the interior.

The Minnesang and Tales of King Arthur: German Literature in the High Middle Ages

by Klaus Kramp

Hartmann von Aue (from the Weingarten Manuscript, first quarter 14th century)
Hartmann von Aue was known in medieval Germany as a writer of both epics and lyrics. The few songs of love and the crusades he wrote are of little consequence compared to his narrative poetry, the most important pieces of which are without doubt "Erec" and "Iwein." The Middle High German book illuminator depicted Hartmann here as a typified knight in full armour, thus identifying the poet as the true creator of Middle High German Arthurian romance.

The ancient Germans had no literature. First and foremost they saw themselves as Teutonic warriors and then, later, as the chivalrous descendants of these warriors; leading the life of writers or scholars was not their idea of life. This meant that up until the middle of the 12th century German literature was exclusively under the influence of monks and the clergy, i.e. the Church. For about four hundred years the only literature written was, with very few exceptions, about spiritual and religious matters. This state of affairs changed abruptly during the last third of the 12th century. This development, like so many of the revolutionary innovations taking place in the 12th and 13th centuries, was a result of the Crusades. Contacts with progressive French culture during the march to the Holy Land and the influence of the political ideas of the Staufer empire led to certain sections of German knighthood feeling that, as far as their education and power went, they were a notch above the rest. The resulting claim to social leadership was expressed not least in attempts to write literature: the knights started speaking out, ousting the clergy from the literary field – and with them religious literature. The following beginning of a short tale reflects the tremendous self-confidence of chivalrous men of letters:

Ein ritter sô gelêret was	A knight was so learned
daz er an den buochen las	that he could read in books
swaz er dar an geschriben vant:	what was written in them.
der was Hartman genant,	He was called Hartmann
dienstman was er zu Ouwe.	and was a *ministerialis*
(From: *Der Arme Heinrich*)	in Aue.

Hartmann von Aue (c. 1160–1210), who wrote this verse in about 1195, introduced a character to German literature who, as no other, symbolizes and embodies chivalry: King Arthur. We know little more about the historical Arthur other than that in about 500 A. D. he led a British army in battle against the Anglo-Saxons. By the middle of the 12th century, there was a wealth of tales and legends focussed on the British army leader, and the French poet Chrétien de Troyes adapted the material at his disposal. He stylized Arthur to become the glorious focal point of a group of knights, the Knights of the Round Table. He is the calm centre of this courtly chivalrous society and embodies the ideal of the exemplary knight and ruler *(rex iustus et pacificus)*. Although the German language has called the literary genre that was born with Chrétien's version of the story the *Artusroman* (Arthurian Romance), the real hero is not Arthur, but the knights gathered round the king at a round table.

Hartmann's Erec, for example, the hero of the first Arthurian romance written in German (c. 1180, based on the Chrétien tale), rides away from King Arthur's court to avenge an insult suffered by Arthur's wife, Queen Ginover (spelt thus in the poem); in the process, he is the glorious victor of a tournament and can thus win the love *(minne)* of Enite. He returns with her to Arthur's court and the wedding is celebrated with great festivity. In the second part of the poem, Erec's love for

Tournament (from a 15th-century manuscript)
Tournaments between knights were the climax of festivals at court and were held as entertainment. Such a tournament consisted not only of "jousting," i. e. a mounted duel, but also of a fight of troop against troop. The lucky winner of a tournament gained a reward of love – often a laurel wreath – and with it the favour of the noble ladies.

his wife makes him neglect his knightly duty to prove his chivalry in battle; he "verligt sich" (sinks into inaction). It is not until Enite secretly laments the disgrace brought upon her by Erec's lack of activity that he remembers his duties. In a whole series of adventures, Erec proves he is worthy of being a knight of the round table, regains his wife's respect and returns to Arthur's court as a celebrated hero. Erec has been able to find self-control *(mâze)*, a harmonious balance between his *minne* (love) of Enite and his *êre* (honour) as a knight.

Erec was Hartmann's first literary work, and its structure is typical of Arthurian romance: riding away from King Arthur's court, a whole series of adventures, successful defence of knightly honour, glorious return. Hartmann's poem, in particular, makes a second aspect clear: Arthurian romance, recited before a knightly and courtly audience, was intended to be more than just exciting entertainment – it was also meant to be didactic. The poet creates for his listeners a world in which chivalrous virtues are idealized. One of the knights, e.g. Erec, is guilty of offending against knightly ethos, and the poet shows how he manages to attain harmony with his estate and his ideals.

Some twenty years passed before Hartmann again turned his attentions to King Arthur and his knights, when, in about 1200, he wrote *Iwein*. Here we again see the hero torn between love and honour. This time, however, love is at a disadvantage, for Iwein gets completely involved in life as a warrior. But here again, after a series of adventures, King Arthur's knight succeeds in regaining his *mâze*. Although *Iwein* is formally and linguistically the most perfect of Hartmann's poetic works, it is nevertheless clear that as far as the contents are concerned it retains the successful concept of the Erec poem.

How does one become one of King Arthur's knights? An answer to this question is given by the first part of the extremely complex and lengthy poem *Parzival* (approx. 25,000 lines in 16 books; written between 1200 and 1210. Its author was Wolfram of Eschenbach (c. 1170–1210). The hero of the story is thirsting for action and so goes out into the world, inspired by a desire to join King Arthur's court. But there are a lot of things he must learn before he can reach his goal, for example that the ideal knight does not fight another – mounted – knight from the ground or pierce him in an unknightly way or even rob him of his armour. Robbing a lady for the sake of a love pledge is certainly not the sort of thing one of Arthur's knights should do, either. Parzival learns his lessons, some of them very painful, proves his knightly worth in battle and finally joins the circle of the knights of the round table. But this is not the end of the road: King Arthur's court is but the first lap on the road to Parzival's true calling. Wolfram sees the true designation of his hero as lying in a God-like, almost spiritual Grail monarchy, which was almost certainly modelled on an order of knights. The second part of the epic poem shows Parzival on his difficult path to the Grail Castle and the Grail, which in Wolfram is a magic stone of religious and mythical significance. He not only joins the *templeisen* (Knights of the Grail), but also becomes their king, because it miraculously turns out at the end of the poem that through his mother he is related to the Grail clan.

Very soon after *Parzival* had been completed, a work critical of the way knighthood had been presenting itself in the Arthurian romances was written. It was *Tristan and Isolde,* a verse romance of some 20,000 lines and written in about 1210. Its author, Gottfried (dates of death and birth are not known), came from the Strasbourg patriciate. He was one of the first people to articulate, if somewhat hesitantly, the claims of the up-and-coming urban bourgeoisie for social equality with the noble knights. That is why Gottfried criticises fighting virtues; in his view, they may certainly impress onlookers, but otherwise they are meaningless. Instead, he emphasises the "inner values" of education and a genteel lifestyle. The tale is intended for a bourgeoisie striving to adapt to the nobility, and although the people in the tale are of noble stock and the action takes place in a courtly milieu (although not at King Arthur's), there are many ways such an audience would be able to identify with the character of Tristan, who is by nature sensitive and artistic.

Events focus on the passionate love between Tristan and Isolde, the wife of King Marke of England – a love triggered off by the accidental drinking of a love potion. This secret, illicit love, people at the king's court jealous of Tristan, a good-natured but suspicious husband – all this leads to numerous complications and a highly dramatic course of events. After King Marke repeatedly catches the lovers *in flagranti,* Tristan has to leave England in a hurry and becomes a mercenary on the continent. The poem is unfortunately unfinished, but further instalments were written (by Ulrich von Türheim, c. 1195–1250, and Heinrich von Freiberg, 1278–1329) and so we know the story was to have had a tragic ending, with Tristan and Isolde dying of a broken heart.

Hartmann, Wolfram and Gottfried incontestably marked the peak of Middle High German epic poetry which, together with Middle High German lyrical poetry, was the most important literary genre of this period. Their poems broke new ground and influenced a great number of less important poets, who continued to write in the same style as the Great Three, gave their works a new treatment or, quite simply, carried

Monk writing (c. 1170)
For almost 400 years, literature in Germany was in the hands of the Church. Copying and illustrating texts was almost exclusively the responsibility of monks in monastery scriptoria. It was not long before centres of painting and writing developed in Germany, such as in Fulda under Hrabanus Maurus or on the Reichenau (Lake Constance). This picture shows the monk Eadwine writing at his desk, laboriously copying a text. Quill and inkhorn are clearly visible.

ILL. PAGES 122–123:
Page of text and an illustration from "Parzival" (beginning of the 13th century)
Apart from the fragmentary "Titurel" and also the uncompleted "Willehalm," the main literary work by Wolfram von Eschenbach was without doubt his "Parzival." The illustration shows three scenes from this long epic poem. At the top we can see a festive table at the court of King Arthur. Some of the people have been identified with a name band. The scene in the middle represents Parzival's fight with his half-brother Feirefiz, and in the bottom sequence Parzival and Feirefiz recognize each other as brothers. Feirefiz has thrown away his sword.

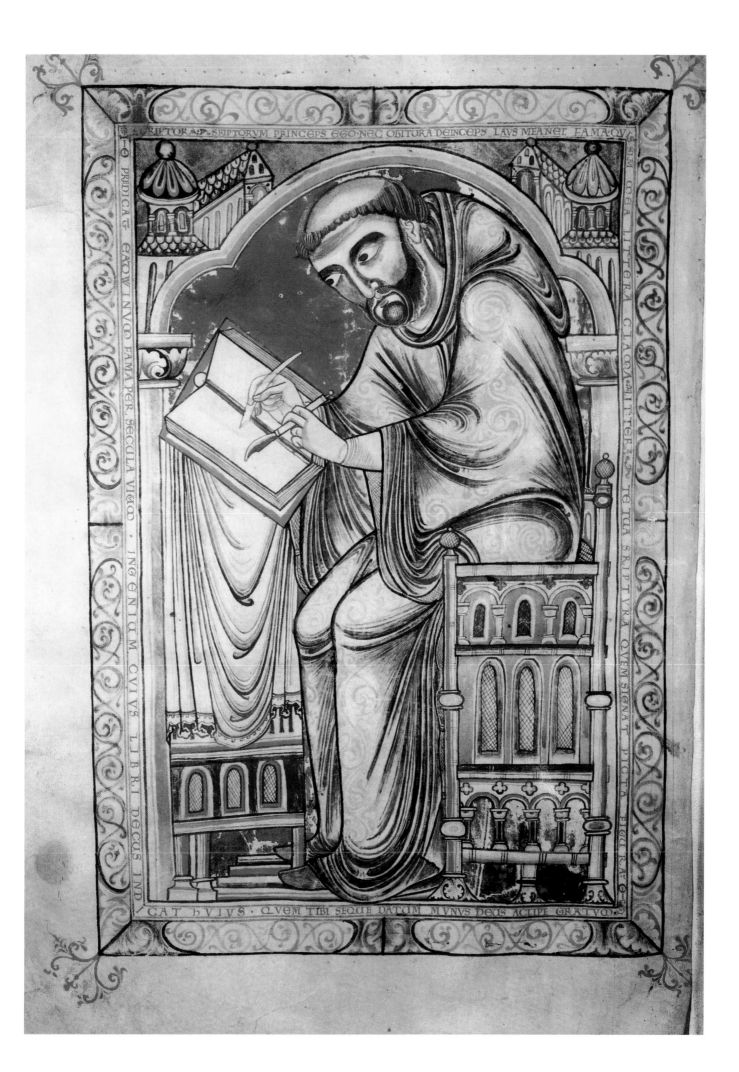

Column 1

herre ir welt gewalt uns an.
sw ir mir grozzen wider saget.
ich bin doch niht so gar verzaget.
ich en bringe ez an ander frage.
ir habet man un mage.
unt den chunch selbe meret.
unser laster generet.
des erwirbe ich uch die hulde.
daz der chunech lat die schulde.
welt ir nach minem rate leben.
unde geselleschaft her vur in geben.
des chunech galmuretes chint.
von un flegen was un ein wint.
der rayel runder hoster bris.
gawan was dirre note alwis.
er heize sich unsanfte erchant.
do er mit dem meter dur die hant.
stach des zwangen minnen chrast.
un wore wiplich geselleschaft.
in selhet von rode ein chungin.
oder chone lehelin.
dr ze einer wiste rich.
in zwanch sus vollecliche.
div senfte sorze wolgevar.
zephande satte ir hoher dar.
do sprach man her gawan.
wel op div minne disen man.
twingt als si mih do zwanch.
un ns sin getrulich gedanch.
der minne mohte ir siges zehen.
e ir mohte des wales sehen.
war stonden div ogen sin.
eine vale von surin.

G gefurret von gelwern zendal.
die swanger uber div bos mal.
do div vale ward der zaher dach.
so daz ir parzival niht sach.
un gap her wider wule sin.
von pelrapeyre div chungin.
div behielt ir doch sin herze dort.

iy rochter horen disiu wort.
er sprach owe minne un wip.
wer hat benomen mir dinen lip.
er warp mit raterschaft man harto.
dine werde minne chrone un zarto.
bin wiel der duch von clamide.
l ofte ich vant ach un we.
unde sufen manch herze sorbel.
in diner helfe dyen nebel.
har dich bi liehter sunnen hue.
wir benomen nune weil ich wre.
er sprach owe wer chom min sper.
daz ich min war brahte her.
do sprach man her gawan.
herre ez ist mir vast vertan.
swen wem sprach der degen wert.
irn trager hie schilt noch daz swert.
wel mohte ich bites an uch belagen.
doch wil ich uwer sporen wagen.
er bet mirz lihte hernach baz.
e swenne ich sich von vast gesaz.
indes ich nimer an uch stru.
doch sint div lant wol so wit.
ich mach da hrus mit arbeit holen.
bi div fride un angest dolen.
ez chunges lores sun do sprach.
swaz hie mir rede gen uch geschach.
daz ist luter un mannehlich.
iho mit valscher trube rich.
ich ger also schel gedienen wil.
hie lw ein chunech un ritter vil.
un wunschlicher frowen schar.
ge selleschaft gibe ich uch dar.
lat mih mit uch riten.
so bewar ich uch vor striten.
ot lone uwer herre ir sprecht wol.
daz ich vil gerne dienen sol.

Column 2

sw uwer companie bret mir.
wer ist uwer herre oder ir.
ich helle herren einen man.
von dem ich manch urbor han.

E ein teil uch der benne hie.
er phlach gein mir des willen ie.
daz er mirz willecliche bot.
sine swester hat der chunch lot.
div mich zer werlde brahte.
swes got an mir gedahte.
daz birt dienst siner hant.
er chunch artus ist er genant.
ich ist min name unverstolen.
an manger stet vil unser holen.
lute die mich erchennent.
gawanen mich die nennent.
iy dient min lip un ich min name.
wel vil ehren mir von schame.
do sprach er bistu gawan.
vil chranchen bris uch des han.
op div mirz wol erburst hie.
ich hore von dir sprechen ie.
dy burest ez allen luten wol.
din dienst ich doch enphahen sol.
iwan uf dinstes gebt.
usage wes sint div gelt.
der mangel ist dort uf geslagen.
lat artus da so muz ich schlagen.
daz ich in mit den ogen min.
y iho mich gesehen noch die chungin.
ich sol rechen noch ein blowen.
daz umbe ich sw mit ruwen.
dir von solhen sachen.
ein wer div maget ir lachen.
iy ir bot die slech der hunschaft.
uir mich daz von ir der gewalt.
unsanfte daz ist gerochen.
sprach gawan un ist zerbrochen.
er leswe arm un daz winster bein.
iw her schowe ors unt den stein.
da legen daz driuzune uf dem sne.
mes spiegel von dem du strazest e.
do parzival die warheit sach.
du daher mer un sprach.
daz laze ich an uch gawan.
op daz si der selbe man.
der mir hat laster vor gelebt.
so rise ich mit dir swar du wrde.
ich nemach gein dir niht liegens phlegen.
sprach gawan hie ist von uost gelegen.
egremors ein strues heto.
des ver gein prise ie was gelebt.
daz was e daz wurde gejalt.
an in beiden halsu bris bezalt.
si raten mit ein ander dan.
er walos un gawan.
vil volches ze orse un zesuz.
ort inne bot un werden groz.
swan un ir zube daz gebot.
gawane un dem reter rot.
gawan cherte da er sin pavelun vant.
fron bunewaren delalant.
er fudre vrile an die sine grench.
si wart fro mit frouden si enphench.
div maget ir ruter der si sach.
daz ir von kei o geschach.
si nam ir bruder un die hant.
unde frun veschuren von tarnant.
suf sach si chomen parzival.
er was gevar durch iser es mal.

A als twere rosen der geflogen.
un was sin har rasch abe gelogen.
er spranch uf do er si chomen sach.
ny hore wie bunewaren sprach.
got alz ez dar nach mir.
willechomen sit daz ir.
b either bi mannelichen siten.
ich here lachen gar vermiten.
uch min herze erchande.
sw mich an frouden phande.

Column 3

kay der mich do so slech.
daz habet gerochen ir gendch.
ich chust uch ware ih chusses were.
des hete ih hivte da gegert.
sprach parzival getorste ih so.
wan ih pin werss chusses fro.
si chusten in satte in nider.
eine unchussowen si sande wider.
unde hiez ir bringen rehte chleu.
uy waren gestrowen alberet.
si phelle von runye.
si sote der chunch clamde.
ir gevangen han gezragen.
div maget si brahte un begunde chlagen.
der mandel ware ane fieder.
kunewar alsus gesser.
yz blancher swe un snoreln.
si zuche un zoch un daz dar in.
oy ir urlobe er sich do troych.
den ram von im der junge troch.
bi roten munde lichzt yel.
gechtet ward der degen snel.
o was er pher un chlar.
swer in sach der iach fur war.
geblomet in vur alle man.
daz lop sin varwe mohte han.
parzivale stont wol sin wat.
eine turen smarat.
spien sun vur sin hobt loch.
uw frowe gap un me doruch.
eine turen gurtel vier.
von edelen stenen manch tier.
iy die ullen of dem borten sin.
div rube was ein rubin.

W wie was der junge ane bart.
geschuher do er gechleider wart.
daz mere guht wolgendch.
daz volch un holdel her ze yich.
bediu man un wip.
die heren wert sinen lip.
er chunch messe hete gehort.
man sach artusen chomen dort.
uw der rayel ander uber.
er schene vaschew nie gerter.
die heren alle e wol vernomen.
der rote ruter ware chomen.
in gawans pavelun.
dar chom artus der brun.
er bedruwen artanor.
spranch dem chunge allez vor.
y riter den walos ersach.
den frager so vil der mich rach.
unde man frowen de lalant.
vil brises guht man werre hant.
kay hat verphendet sin dron ist ny gelendet.
ich furht wench sinen swench.
der teswe arm ir un lechranch.
do sprach der junge parzival.
ane fluge engels mal.
suf geblomet of der erden.
artus mit den werden.
e nphench in ruterliche.
des willen waren riche.
alle die in sahen da.
ir herzen volge div sprach ia.
ein sinem lobe sprach niemen nein.
so rehte munchlicher schein.
artus sprach zeim san.
ir habet mir liep un leit getan.
doch haber ur mir der ere.
brahte un gesendet mere.
danne ih uz ie von manne enphench.
un dienst da gein noch chleine grench.
het ir brises niht me getan.
wan daz div her zogin sol han.
si reschure die hulde.
dch war uch kay schulde.
gewandet un gesprochen.
et ich uch e gesprochen.

ILL. PAGE 124:
"Minne" scene (Grosse Heidelberger Liederhandschrift, beginning of 14th century) The adored lady is giving the Minnesinger a wreath as a sign of her favour. And yet the "frouwe" is not making it all that easy for him to reap the just reward of his singing – he has to climb a long ladder to reach the lady's chamber. That this is really quite a courageous undertaking for the knight is indicated by the fact that the onlooker cannot see how many rungs of the ladder the singer has already climbed: he seems to be balanced high up in the air.

ILL. PAGE 125:
Fighting scene (Grosse Heidelberger Liederhandschrift, beginning of 14th century) The life of a knight was largely dominated by fighting. The Middle High German tales of King Arthur describe in detail many battle scenes from which the hero emerges victorious. Our picture shows the bitter struggle for a town. On the battlements, the ladies are fearfully watching the turmoil on the battlefield.

Social Life (Grosse Heidelberger Liederhandschrift, beginning 14th century) Minnesang was a social art. The singer performed his song before an aristocratic audience, thus introducing variety to the daily routine of knights and their ladies at court. Very often the singer was himself part of the noble or knightly circle at a particular castle and in his song made allusions to certain people and events, which lent a degree of spiciness to his presentation. As we can see in the picture on the left, most minnesongs were accompanied by a musical instrument, such as fiddle, harp or bagpipes.

on where they had left off. Poets like Ulrich von Zazikhoven or Wirnt von Grafenberg increasingly displayed an urge to write texts that were nothing if not entertaining; didactic aims are neglected for the sake of an exciting story. From the first line, heroes like Ulrich's Lanzelet or Wirnt's Wigalois are not bothered by problems or a bad conscience. They go through life without blemish or blame, leading an existence that is heroic to the core. The fairy-tale world of the Arthurian romances is filled with ever more dreadful monsters and fabulous beings that only seem to be waiting for Lanzelet or Wigalois, or whatever these heroes are called, to put an end to them. This is the beginning of the fantasy novel.

The influence of French art and the Romance spirit came much later to the region that is now Austria than it did to the rest of the area ruled by the Staufer. This made it much easier for local material and Germanic heroic legends to be taken up by literary writers. The *Nibelungenlied*, written in 2,379 four-line stanzas by an unknown poet about 1200, came at the end of a long chain of versions handed down by word of mouth. Basically, this epic poem deals with historical material, and as a result it is more realistic than the Arthurian romances. In part one, we are told about Siegfried, who succeeds in defeating in a fight Brunhild, who is said to be unvanquishable, thus winning her hand for the Burgundian king Gunther; in return, he gains Gunther's sister Kriemhild as his wife. Jealousy between Brunhild and Kriemhild leads to Siegfried's death. From now on, Kriemhild's life is dominated by one thought – taking revenge on the Burgundians for Siegfried's death. The second part of the *Nibelungenlied* shows how Kriemhild succeeds in bringing about the downfall of the Burgundians, thus quenching her excessive thirst for revenge.

About the same time as the Arthurian romances there developed the courtly love lyric known as *Minnesang*. When we speak of lyric poetry in this context, we mean something entirely different from what is meant today. Nowadays, poetry is generally something we read to ourselves in the privacy of our own four walls, perhaps even by the romantic glow of candlelight. In the Middle Ages, however, lyric poetry was performed as songs before a courtly, chivalric audience. *Minnesang* is not based on personal experience. Rather, it is centred on the role of the characters in it and moves along paths that are rigidly adhered to. The roles of women and of men alike are clearly defined. The lady *(frouwe)*, often the (already married) lady of the castle, is seen as the embodiment of beauty. Her main task is to effect the ennoblement of the man's character, to make him "golde gelîch" (= like gold), as the Burggraf von Rietenburg puts it. The singer's aim is to win the lady's favor. Paradoxically – and this is very difficult for people nowadays to understand – the singer by no means expects his romantic yearnings to be requited, for only if the lady remains at a distance, unattainable for him, can she carry out her didactic, moral task.

Initially, the roles of the singer and his *frouwe* were not governed by such rigid rules. In the early period of the *Minnesang* (approx. 1150–1180) the *frouwe* sometimes appears in the role of the wooer, while the knight renounces her, thus attracting her excessive anger, such as in the following verse from the *Kürenbergers* (mid-12th century):

Jô stuont ich nehtint spâte   vor dînem bette.
dô getorste ich dich, frouwe,   niwet wecken.
'des gehazze iemer   got den dînen lîp
jô enwas ich niht ein eber   wilde', sô sprach daz wîp.

Walther von der Vogelweide (from the "Weingartner Liederhandschrift," 1st quarter 14th century) Walther von der Vogelweide was the first poet writing in German who, in his so-called "Sprüche," or political songs and poems, referred to contemporary political events. The three "Reichssprüche" he wrote between 1198 and 1201 not only describe the turmoil connected with the struggle for the throne after the death of Henry VI (1197); they also appeal for unity and order. The above picture illustrates the first of these poems:
Ich saz ûf eime steine
und dahte bein mit beine:
darûf satzt ich den ellenbogen
ich hete in mîne hant gesmogen
daz kinne und ein mîn wange.
(Roughly: I sat on a stone
and crossed one leg over the other:
I put my elbow on it
And cupped in my hand
my chin and one of my cheeks.)

Roughly: (He:) Truly, I was standing at your bed yesterday evening.
But mistress, I didn't dare wake you.
(She:) May God hate you forever for that!
Truly, I wasn't a wild boar, spake the woman.

The (sexual) fulfilment of love is still a subject dealt with by poetry in these early days and is unabashedly spoken about:
ab zoch er den mantel sein, er warfft in in das grass.
da lagen die zway die langen nacht, piss an den liechten tag.
Roughly: He took his coat off, he threw it into the grass,
and so the two of them lay there all night until the light of day.
(*Kerensteinballade*)

But then the influence of the French art of poetry very soon starts making itself felt in German lyric poetry. From now on, the lady is obligated to take the part of the one who turns away her wooer, while the man yearns in vain. The lyrical language becomes more subtle, the meetings of *frouwe* and *man* are reduced to a few typical situations. The only freedom of choice the poet has is in the form of the verses, lyrical images and similes. When *Minnesang* was at its height (approx. 1180–1230) it became an art of variation.

By far the most colourful personality of the *Minnesang* poets was Walther von der Vogelweide (c. 1170–1230). In his *Tristan*, Gottfried von Strassburg sings his praises as the unequivocal leader of the "nightingales" (Minnesingers) and places the poets' crown on his head. Walther learnt the art of Minnesang from *Reinmar the Elder*, one of the leading Minnesingers of the period, in around 1190. He soon freed himself from his teacher and developed his own unmistakable style, which is above all characterised by his attempts to free the Minnesang from its rigid conventions by making it truer to life. He wrote extensively (approx. 80 lyric poems); in his work the lady is toppled from her excessively high pedestal and becomes more realistic, more life-like, more like women really were. Requited love is now possible, although the lady of noble stock is replaced by a girl of lower status. Songs like "Unter der Linde auf der Heide" and "Nehmt, frouwe, diesen Kranz" with their folkish character have remained alive over the centuries. Until the age of 50, Walther led a wandering life that took him to the various European courts. This is where his *Sprüche* – political songs and poems – originated, in which he supports the idea of a strong emperor against the pope, for example in "Ich saz ûf eime steine." Walther was thus the first poet writing in German to comment on political events of the day.

The same unease that Walther must have felt towards the bloodlessness of the *Minnesang* led Neidhart von Reuental (1190–1246) to begin a positively revolutionary revival of court poetry. He introduced the peasant into the *Minnesang* (known now as *Dörperdichtung*). The courtly knight and his *frouwe* are replaced by the country squire, peasants and a country wench *(frouwelîn)*, the scene of action taken from the castle into the village. At a dance a landed nobleman woos the favour of one of the village girls, but finds himself competing with the peasants. The result is a jolly good punch-up, at the end of which the nobleman is often rather the worse for wear. This is one of the standard situations in Neidhart's songs. The other one is a mother trying to stop her daughter from going dancing. The daughter gets her own way, goes to the dance and is the cause of a dispute between a nobleman and peasants. Here again, the whole thing ends up with a free-for-all. In spite of their contents,

Village dance (end of 15th century)
Even today we do not exactly know what circumstances led to the development of minnesang. One of the various theories says that minnesang went back to popular dancing and love songs. It is thought the following short dancing song (from "Carmina Burana") is possibly a forerunner of what later became the lyrics of knights:

Swaz hie gât umbe,
daz sint alle megede,
die wellent ân man,
allen diesen sumer gân.
(Roughly: The people going round in a circle
Are all girls;
They want to stay without a man
All this summer.)

Neidhart's songs were not written for the peasants, but for knights at court – and they must have had a lot of fun from these crude jokes.

It is not without reason that Neidhart has been called the "gravedigger of the *Minnesang*." True, the *Minnesang* was still around until the 16th century – from 1300 we speak of the *Meistersang*, because poems were written by master craftsmen such as Hans Sachs – but with Neidhart's *Dörperdichtung* at the latest, songs of chivalry noticeably started going into decline. *Minnesang* and Arthurian romance were the main genres of Middle High German literature until the social upheavals of the 14th century. They are an expression of the culture of the age of chivalry – a culture that lost its importance as the concept the nobility had of itself changed and with the growth of the wealth and power of the urban bourgeoisie.

Modes of Thought and Consciousness in the High Middle Ages

by Günter Meller

Lecture at a university (wood engraving, beginning 16th century)

A growing need for knowledge that could not be fulfilled by cathedral or monastery schools led to the establishment of the first universities in the Middle Ages. These universities were unions of private academic schools which had gradually been given more and more privileges by the emperor or pope (e. g. academic freedom, statutory autonomy, freedom from tax, own jurisdiction). The most important of the medieval universities was Paris (founded 1253), on which the earliest German universities, dating back to the 14th century, were modelled: Prague university, founded by Charles IV, Vienna founded in 1365, Heidelberg in 1386 and Cologne in 1388.

Dieter Kühn, in his book on the Middle High German poet Wolfram von Eschenbach[1], makes an interesting experiment. He himself, a 20th century writer with a good knowledge of history, describes a journey that takes him both from the Eifel near the Belgian-German border down to Eschenbach in southern Germany and, at the same time, down through the centuries back into the High Middle Ages. The exciting thing about this trip is the attempt to see the world as someone living then would have done. Once he has arrived in the High Middle Ages, our modern writer has become a *ministerialis*, a member of the lower nobility. Bligger is his name. He is woken by the call of the night watchman announcing the approaching dawn. Next to him, almost in a sitting position in a short bed, is his wife, and there are four children lying asleep on cushions on the floor. His imagination starts wandering and he thinks that really it is not the night watchman that should be waking him, but his *frouwe*, i.e. not his own wife, but the wife of a knight. She should wake him with a kiss, for he must be off before other early risers notice he was with this woman while her husband was away on his lord's business.

Itinerant singers have introduced Bligger to the literature of the period that is having such an effect on his imagination. He wonders about which wife of which knight in the area he could be woken by in this manner in the morning. Certainly, he's already got a lover – a young wench of low status, as is befitting of his station in life. He's meeting her that very afternoon in the bath house. But that's not the kind of love a monk from a neighbouring monastery told him he'd read about in a book he was copying. Ah, such neverending love of a lady of noble stock – that'd be the thing, thinks Dieter Kühn's Bligger. Why is Bligger dreaming of such a love? What does he think of his own marriage?

At this point, the author interrupts his narrative. He does not want to describe something fictitious, something there are no documents about dating back to the period in question. Virtually nothing is known about the feelings husband and wife had for each other. In fact, there is very little to be found out about the personal, individual traits – thoughts, feelings – of someone living in the Middle Ages. All portrayals and descriptions of individual people, both in the fine arts and in literature, have something stylised and general about them. Can we conclude from this that people living in the Middle Ages could not differentiate between the world of their minds and the outside world, that their consciousness of themselves as individuals was less marked than it is today? Did they in that case have less of a rational distance both to the real world around them and to the subjective world of their minds? Such a supposition certainly seems possible.

It is supported by Norbert Elias at the end of an introduction to mediaeval etiquette. In instructions in table manners dating from this period, written for people belonging to the upper class, he found instructions like "Don't clean your teeth with your knife," "Don't spit on the table," "Don't offer someone else the remains of your soup or bread

The seven liberal arts (from the "Hortus Delicarium," 12th century)
Medieval studies were ordered according to the seven liberal arts ("artes liberales"). They were called liberal arts because in ancient Rome only the "liberi," i. e. free men, were allowed to pursue them. The number seven was stipulated by Augustinus (354–430) – the "trivium" comprising the disciplines grammar, rhetoric and logic, and the "quadrivium" with the mathematical sciences of music, geometry, arithmetic and astronomy.

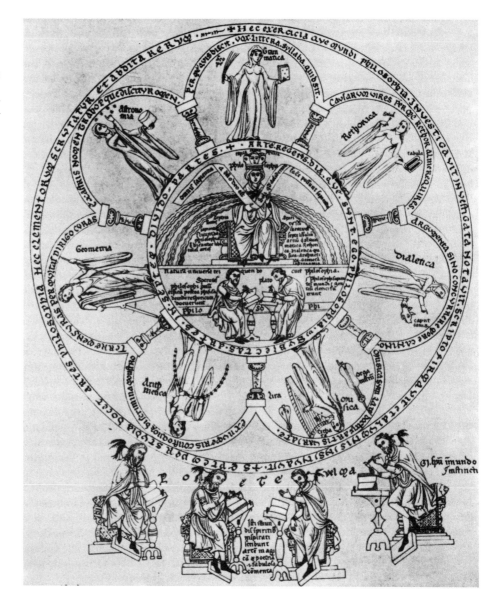

you've already bitten bits off," "Don't throw bones you've been gnawing back into the communal pot," and others like these. Elias closely connects the standard of behaviour suggested by these rules of etiquette with human relations and the peculiarities of emotional life, which in those days were so very different ours today: "People who ate together in the way that was the custom in the Middle Ages ... had a very different relationship to each other than we do today, not only on the level of their clear and precisely understood consciousness; it seems that their emotional life had a different structure and different character. Their emotions were conditioned to forms of relationships and behaviour that today would be felt to be embarrassing or, at the very least, not very attractive."[2] Elias says that the "embarrasment threshold" and "limit of shame" of the people of the Middle Ages were on a very different level to ours. That is, they had less control of their emotions than we do. We can perhaps connect what is being said here about the character of emotionality with the supposition we mentioned above: People living in the Middle Ages had less of a rational distance both to the real world around them and to the subjective world of their minds. Things we are more likely to see as ideas, concepts and principles were for them objective facts, i.e. they really existed, such as demons, devils, cardinal virtues and cardinal vices. On the other hand, outside things – a

Mappa mundi (11th century)
In the Middle Ages, Latin cartography was universal cartography, i. e. the earth was always shown as a whole. The main purpose of medieval maps was to explain the Bible by documenting God's deeds of salvation on earth. The earth had a predetermined form which only needed to be filled in by the map-maker. The most common form was the T-map (see above): the three continents then known, Asia, Europe and Africa, were arranged like a T in a circle. Asia was put in the upper half, Europe in the quarter on the left, Africa on the right, and water separated the continents from each other. As a rule, East was at the top of the map; only the ancient Greeks put North at the top, while the Arabs had South at the top.

courtly gesture, a farting pig that could cause endless mirth, a belt decorated with gold that one just had to have – these they experienced so powerfully that they dominated their innermost being.

The mediaeval concept of space and time was very different to ours, and this indeed tells us a lot about the peculiarities of the way people in those days thought. Nowadays, as the result of the ubiquitousness of clocks, we are so used to measuring time exactly that we can hardly imagine basing our feeling for time on other factors. The same is true of space, which in our day and age is cartographically measured, allowing us to locate various positions in our mind's eye and connect them with a line. Yards and miles, metres and kilometers, and over a certain distance light years – these are the units we know nowadays. Light years are obviously too much for even our modern imagination to cope with, but the fact that we can, as a matter of course, use such abstract terms is typical of the way we view time and space compared to earlier centuries, when the act of measuring and the units used were directly connected to the work and experiences of the people.

By the Middle Ages, sun dials and water clocks had already been invented, and from the 13th century on there were mechanical clocks run by clockwork. In spite of this, people mainly read the time from the position of the sun, the sequence of day and night, the fulness of the moon (months) and the change of the seasons. In monasteries, the day was also divided up by hourly (horary) prayers. These small social units in particular had a greater need of precise divisions of time, which, among other things, had the function of bringing order into life. The fact that in the agrarian society of the Middle Ages time was largely measured by natural events also had an effect on the specific structure of human consciousness. The perpetual return of the same events in the cycle of nature affected, for example, certain attitudes: "Not change but repetition was the determining factor of people's mind and behaviour. For them something that happened once, something they had never seen before, had no instrinsic value... Archaic society negated individuality and unusual behaviour. It was the norm, even a virtue, to behave as everyone else did, to behave as people always had done. Only such traditional behaviour possessed moral strength."[3]

In the Middle Ages, the close relation of people with nature affected their view of space. This relationship was marked neither by an impersonal view nor by contemplative observation; rather it was down-to-earth activity in the fields. It was in their bodies and in their work that people found their criteria for measuring space. The length of a path was measured not with abstract units, but in paces; other commonly used measurements were feet, ell (corresponded to the length of the lower arm between elbow and wrist, after the German word for the ulna), span, and finger. The word "Morgen" not only meant "morning," but also the amount of land that could be ploughed in that period of time. Over and above these basic measurements, the concept of space caused great difficulty. Descriptions of how to get somewhere usually ended up as accounts of experiences at points along the way. Whenever the concept of space left the direct range of human experience, as for example is the case beyond matters of this earth, God and His plan of salvation for the earth replaced man as the measure of all things.

The representation of space in the fine arts shares this Christian reference. The aim of painting of the High Middle Ages is not to put objects into the correct perspective, but rather to emphasize important elements. If, for example, the door is the important part of a house, then the door is drawn disproportionately large, perhaps surrounded by the outline of a little play house. A detail could be symbolic of the whole. The space surrounding an object or person was often depicted as a ray of bright light falling to earth from the face of God. Happenings on earth were, so to speak, included in the goodness and warmth of God. "Space is nothing more than the brightest light," mystics declared. "Below" and "above" are more than just abstract details of space and position. "Below" is where hell is and devils and purgatory, and "above" is where heaven is, with God in His majesty and angels making music all around Him. The world was the entirety of the farmsteads, the universe rather like a human body enlarged to gigantic proportions. In the Middle Ages, thinking in terms of space was a symbolic process dominated by experience. There was also a certain magic about places, and, for example, crimes committed near religious places carried the heaviest penalties.

In the Middle Ages, this non-abstract concept of space and time was closely related to the prevalent innumeracy. Most people were unable to read and write, and geometry and algebra were way beyond their comprehension. Even the learned monks on Reichenau Island in Lake Constance, for example, failed in their attempts to draw a plan of the monastery garden. They racked their brains, but it was just too much for them to imagine the rear boundary of their garden running at an angle to a stream. The conundrum was worth making into a competition: How was it possible for the transverse paths to run parallel to the rear wall and still cross the main path at right angles? The answer lay in pulling down the rear wall to solve the problem of the oblique garden beds. Another competition was about whether two times one hundred could be divided into three parts. This question turned out to be unanswerable. The monks counted and counted, but 200 was just too much. It was not possible for them to do arithmetic in writing using Roman figures. They had abacuses with which they tried to put the ones, tens and hundreds into order before adding them up. But multiplication and division were not possible with this aid. It was not until Adam Riese wrote his arithmetic books that Arab figures started being commonly used, thus making it possible to work with the decimal system in writing. Figures usually just had symbolic significance. They spoke of 11,000 virgins being killed or of 100,000 heroes slain. But all these figures meant was that it was a very large number.

From what we have seen so far, mediaeval thought can be briefly summed up as follows: Thought was dominated by concrete concepts. All things in the world, all thoughts seemed to be significantly related to each other. The central perspective that informed and governed life was the presence and influence of God, and it gave everything in the world its place and determined its task. Mediaeval thought was very one-track: analysis, abstraction, rational distance – all these had scarcely been developed. Viewing something for its own sake, to take it out of context and, above all, see it in a neutral light without relating it to religion caused insuperable difficulties. Indeed, it was completely out of the question.

In view of this conclusion, we might be tempted to say that the weaknesses and difficulties mentioned were the result of intellectual inability. There is no doubt about it that then most people had no regular schooling and therefore the level of their elementary knowledge of the world was low compared to today. But that does not mean to say we can

Cosmos man (miniature from Hildegard of Bingen's "Revelationes," first half of the 13th century) The Middle Ages saw man as a microcosm, i. e. as an image of the visible world on a smaller scale. Isidor of Seville described the relation of man and world as follows: "In a supranatural sense, the world is fittingly called man. For in the same way that the world comprises four elements, man comprises four humours (temperaments) in a certain proportion to each other. That is why the ancient peoples connected man with the creation of the world, which in Greek is called cosmos, but man is called microcosm, i. e. smaller world . . ."

Alma mater (from a medieval manuscript in the Vatican library)
Medieval universities consisted of two faculties – an upper one with the disciplines theology, medicine and jurisprudence, and a lower one, the "faculty of arts." The faculty of arts comprised the seven liberal arts and was a precondition for attending the upper faculty. Tuition was held in Latin and covered "lectiones" (lectures) and "disputationes" (discussions). After studying at the arts faculty, students were awarded the academic degree of "baccalaureus"; the degree of "licentiatus," "magister" or "doctor" was awarded to students who had attended the higher faculty.

doubt their basic intellectual capabilities. Before we start supposing them in some way deficient, it must be made clear that life in the High Middle Ages functioned differently from today, that it was dominated by Christian faith and that in connection with this the methods of verifying thought processes were completely different from today's. Of course, in those days, too, statements about the world, judgements about right and wrong could be true or false. Therefore it was necessary for them to be verified. In most cases, this expression was more appropriate than "proving" them. (Proof, in the sense of logical deduction and rational argumentation, was provided mostly by theologians and philosophers at the universities, who from the 13th century increasingly dominated European thought. There will be more about these scholars later.)

Verification was a matter of tradition and of writing. Writing was something that would survive, that was permanent, and as such was reliable. This reliability largely came from the Holy Scripture, the Bible, but it also came from early (late classical) interpreters and defenders of Christian teachings, the Church Fathers (especially Augustine), who enjoyed a high degree of authority. For centuries it sufficed to refer to them as the main witnesses of an unadulterated Church tradition: Dogmatic controversies were not settled with arguments, but with quotations. Reference to the Church Fathers was an expression of the traditional concept of their spiritual "fatherhood"; recognition of their authority was based on respect, trust and obedience – all of which are attitudes that have since lost their significance in our understanding of science and scholarliness.

The fact that something was documented in writing and had the seal of authorized persons affixed to it gave great weight to the validity of Church decrees and the laws of temporal leaders. This tempted scribes and copiers of such documents – for various reasons – to forge them. The Middle Ages was a heyday for forgeries (the most famous example is the Donation of Constantine). There are big names among the people involved, including bishops and even popes; indeed, the majority of forgeries were done by the clergy. This is amazing – and yet again it is not if we bear in mind that the clergy were, in the main, the only people able to read and write. The reasons why forgeries were made also relativize this statement. A study of mediaeval forgery practices reveals a lot about the state of mind of people then. The historian Horst Fuhrmann has compiled some interesting data which tell us a little about the mediaeval concept of law. Let us look at them more closely.[4]

Mediaeval moral philosophy, following the teachings of Augustine, rejected all forms of forgery. Some historians, in view of this clear position and the fact that in practice it was often not adhered to, have spoken of a blatant lack of morality in the Middle Ages. Fuhrmann has countered this clear-spoken evaluation by asking what forgery really is. What he wants to do is show that, because of a different understanding of law in the Middle Ages, the offence of forgery was to be judged differently than it is today. Nowadays, law is understood to be norms that have been legally established and written down in law books. Such a positive concept of law was unknown in the Middle Ages. "Law was understood to be something with a higher meaning independent of human statutes. Law and justice were one and the same ... A law endowed with the spirit of equity was the same as a just judgement. This equity was both personally felt justice and general morality in one."[5]

In the Middle Ages, therefore, it was certainly possible to forge
something with the knowledge that it would serve justice or salvation. A
legal text would be rewritten with the intention of emphasising the good
aspects of a law that might have been obscured by its wording; passages
were deleted perhaps with the intention of bringing a regulation up to
date or adapting it to regional peculiarities. We can often assume that
"good" intentions of such a nature lay behind alterations, especially
when personal or party interests in a forgery can be excluded. If we
disregard forgeries for personal gain – and these were by no means
uncommon – we can see from these forgeries made in the service of
justice that in the Middle Ages the spirit was more important than the
letter and that was the reason why they did not take the accuracy of the
wording too seriously. Fuhrmann also sees in this attitude an important

Albertus Magnus (Hans Holbein the Elder, High Altar of the former Dominican monastery in Frankfurt/Main, 1501)
Albertus Magnus (c. 1200–1280), a scientist, philosopher and theologian known as "doctor universalis" for the great breadth of his knowledge and intellectual interest, came from a Staufer *ministerialis* family. He joined the Dominican Order in 1229, and between 1242 and 1248 taught in Paris and then in Germany (inter alia 1248–1254 in Cologne). His main significance for medieval philosophy lay in his research and dissemination of Aristotelian, Arab and Jewish writings.

reason why forgeries often remained undetected: It was not particularly important if a document was genuine or not as long as it was imbued with the spirit of God.

Texts were treated allegorically and interpreted from a Christian point of view, which corresponded to the Christian and symbolic way reality was faced. Another example of this was the mediaeval concept of history. Although chronicles had been written, it was not known how long ago in terms of years and days the events chronicled had taken place. People did not know how old they were, or they knew only vaguely. And it didn't really matter. To them the past was also the present, for the nature of things did not change. It was impossible to imagine thought patterns and behaviour different from their own. For them, Jesus and his apostles were journeying or feasting knights just like Dietrich von Bern or King Arthur. Characters from the Bible were always depicted as contemporaries. In the early – pagan – Middle Ages, the people would count the generations, only taking the most important ancestors into account as they did so. In this way, it did not take long for them to get back to the history of the gods: the seventh or eighth ancestor of an early mediaeval German king was already a god or demigod. In the High Middle Ages, it was increasingly believed that the birth of Jesus divided historic time into two parts. His birth was the year zero and the central point of time. This date was an historical axis: Historical figures and events from the post-Jesus age corresponded to figures and events in the pre-Jesus age. Here again we see the influence of a deep-felt need to create connecting links between events – after all, even the order of things created by God had to be based on history.

This historical inability of people of the Middle Ages to imagine the peculiarities of another age was also true when it came to dealing with strangers in their own day. They were scarcely able to understand someone else's individual traits. Strange characteristics (of a stranger) were monstrous, to be laughed at or feared. The paradox of stupidity operated here: If you did not understand, you had already understood everything. What was missing was critical detachment, a knowledge of one's lack of knowledge. The dialectics of not understanding caused mediaeval man to make projections: He recognised someone else only in as far as he thought he saw himself. This is indeed a shortcoming – not in intelligence, but in an ability to reflect.

But where and how could mediaeval man have learned to reflect? He would have had to have learned to observe without prejudice and ask his own detailed questions. But hardly anyone was able to ask questions. The questions in learned conversations, and in schoolbooks the questions asked were mainly traditional and to be answered with definitions learned by heart. Learning in the Middle Ages meant learning traditional material by heart. Even in the disputes of learned thinkers at universities there prevailed a certain pattern of thought – the syllogism, e.g. all men called Gaius are Romans, this man is called Gaius, thus . . . A definition was given, an individual case was assigned to it, an inference drawn. Methodical thinking followed the old tradition of rhetoric and was deductive, i.e. particular ideas deduced from general ideas. The reverse, inductive procedure, i.e. using individual cases to draw up a rule, was out of the question. Neither did mediaeval thinkers proceed pragmatically, as Aristotle had recommended they should for many questions. In the introduction to his *Tropica*, Aristotle had said that there were also probable and accepted principles if their truth could not be

Plague procession (detail of a miniature in the "Très Riches Heures," beginning of 15th century) People in the Middle Ages were powerless in the face of sickness, epidemics and death. Only belief in a life after death made fear of dying bearable for these pious Christians. If they were befallen by a big epidemic, such as the bubonic plague in the 14th century, which wiped out a quarter of the population of Europe, they took it as divine punishment. The result was a number of fanatic forms of religious penance, such as flagellations, satanic cults, superstition, not to mention a feeling of helplessness, anger and despair.

deducted. That which most people regard as being probable, and which at the same time appears probable to scholars or the majority of the best, is probable. There were just not the institutional preconditions for this pragmatic approach. There were no forums for discussions to weigh arguments up and deliberate on them. Truth was indivisible – controversies had to be concluded immediately and in a fighting spirit. Mediaeval thought did not make itself the subject of thought.

This summary of the style of thought of those educated at monastery and cathedral schools applies to common practice and the theological and philosophical mean. Prominent mediaeval philosophers like Anselm of Canterbury, Peter Abelard, Albertus Magnus and especially Thomas Aquinas need to be described in greater detail and evaluated differently. Mediaeval philosophy as a whole does not have a reputation of having brought forth important ideas or even influential innovations for the following centuries. It is therefore not easy to do it justice. Hegel, in his lectures on the history of philosophy, called them "both extensive and meagre, terribly badly written and voluminous"[6].

But here again, we must take a relative view: Scholasticism was something new in that it dominated the spirit of the universities founded in the 13th century and represented this spirit through these new institutions. Its relation to tradition was not to be equated with that believing trust in the Church Fathers prevailing in monastery and cathedral schools. In the case of scholasticism, relation to tradition meant the acceptance and acquisition of classical philosophy, especially Aristotelianism, and the pervasiveness of the theology of the Church Fathers. The very fact that scholasticism was basically conceptual meant it was critical of the symbolic, pictorial and metaphorical thought of the period. Nowadays, we find very strange the "school-like" aspects of mediaeval philosophy – even the word "scholastic" emphasises this. It can be explained by the fact "that, more than anything else, it was an unprecedented learning process, a school event of enormous proportions that continued over the centuries."[7] Mediaeval philosophy was "terribly badly written" (as Hegel saw it) precisely because it regarded its task as arranging the assimilated legacy of the classical world from the

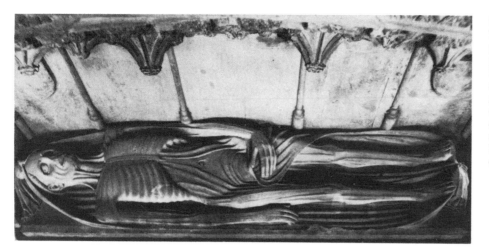

Gravestone of a canon
The terrible and agonizing experience of the plague considerably increased the already strongly pronounced feeling of medieval men and women that life could cease at any moment. Hitherto, the aim of gravestone sculptures had mainly been to give an idealised and artistic reproduction of the dead person as a reminder of their deeds and achievements during their lifetime. But then a realistic and naturalistic style of representation began to dominate, which impressively documented their fear of death.

point of view of how well it could be taught and learned. This was a very down-to-earth business which, naturally enough, neglected the interesting element of personal immediacy.

The identification of scholasticism with mediaeval philosophy is really an inadmissable modification of the word. Rather, scholasticism is used for scholarly activity generally in the High Middle Ages. Medicine, jurisprudence, theology – incidentally, where is the line to be drawn between philosophy and theology? – are all influenced by the scholastic form of presentation of the arguments. This form is not just limited to the presentation of scholarly texts; it is also a characteristic stylistic element of the inner scholastic discussion: Firstly, the arguments of a problem are listed and evaluated. "The scholarly result is reached by means of an extensive documentation of the arguments and criticism thereof. At the end there is the determination by the magister: This is the outline of systematic disputation and is also the literary form of the quaestio, in which the process of forming a scholarly judgement is presented most appropriately."[8]

It is largely due to the translations and commentaries written by mediaeval philosophers that classical works, particularly the very influential writings of Aristotle and his followers, were passed on and made known. Anicius Manlius, a Roman statesman, scholar and philosopher living right at the beginning of the Middle Ages (c. A.D. 480–A.D. 524) and better known as Boethius, is particularly worth mentioning. He had made it his goal to translate into Latin and interpret all the works of Plato and Aristotle he could lay his hands on. Certainly, he did not get beyond some of Aristotle's scripts on logic, but it was precisely these that had an extremely great influence on mediaeval philosophy. The heyday of the dissemination of Aristotle was in the century between 1150 and 1250. Dissemination came about through contacts with oriental culture, mainly via the Crusades and the Moorish rule in Spain. Both the Arabic and the Jewish scholarly traditions had retained the legacy of Greek thought directly and more completely than monasteries in the West. Thus, most of Aristotle's works, including not only those on logic, but also the essential parts of his philosophical writings, were at last translated from Arabic into Latin. It was particularly challenging for the Christian world of the West to assimilate the most highly developed philosophical system of the classical world, a system that had already been given a systematic and non-Christian interpretation and had been precisely articulated.

The Dominican monk Albertus Magnus (1200–1280) succeeded in realizing the plan of Boethius, 700 years after the latter's death. He wrote commentaries on the entire works of Aristotle. In addition, his own writings were so extensive that it would be legitimate to call him "the Great" simply on the grounds of the unparalleled wealth of material he wrote or collected. After studying theology, he spent ten years teaching in various monasteries in Germany. In 1242, he was the first German to be given a chair in Paris, the leading and most famous university of the day. It was here that he met his most famous student, the 20-year-old Thomas Aquinas from Naples. He had been born in 1225 near Naples, the youngest son of a distinguished noble family. Against the bitter resistance of his family, who held him captive for over a year, he joined the Dominican order at the age of 18. He started his studies in Paris and Cologne in 1248, and Albertus Magnus was one of his teachers. In 1257 he gained the title and privileges of master of theology. Thomas Aquinas taught in Paris and various other places in Italy until his death in 1274.

In contrast to Albertus Magnus, who also as a writer of scientific books had a stronger tendency towards empiricism and, in view of the extent of his works, collecting material, Thomas Aquinas had a great gift of penetrating, shaping and ordering his themes. In his famous "summae" or personal syntheses (the "Summa contra gentiles" and "Summa theologiae") and his numerous "questionae" he is regarded by many people as being the greatest theologian and philosopher in the High Middle Ages. This view would seem to be objectively justified in that Thomas Aquinas, as no other before or after him, succeeded in joining *fides* and *ratio*, belief and reason. "Link, as much as you can, belief and reason" – this principle laid down by Boethius put into words the task of the whole of mediaeval philosophy. "Bring what you believe into a new, meaningful attribution, to the ceaseless and immeasurably multiplying entirety of the natural knowledge of man and the world."[9]

Let us look at the following quotation by Thomas Aquinas as an example of the way a didactic play is treated in the High Middle Ages. The numerous proofs of God illustrate in a special way attempts to link *fides* and *ratio*.

"We can say that the fact that God is can be proved in five different ways. The first and most obvious way, however, is that which comes from movement. It is certain and manifest that some things in this world are moved. Everything that is moved is moved by something else. For nothing is moved unless it is possible for it to be moved. But something moves providing it is in reality; for moving means nothing more than taking something out of the sphere of possibility and transferring it into the sphere of reality. But something cannot be transferred from possibility except by something being in reality: e.g. something hot in reality, such as fire, causes wood, which is hot according to possibility, to become hot in reality, and so it moves it and changes it. But it is not possible that the same thing is reality and possibility at the same time in the same way, but only in different ways: that which is hot in reality cannot be simultaneously hot in possibility, but is cold in possibility. It is thus impossible that something is moving and is moved or moves itself in the same way. Thus everything that moves must be moved by something else. If that which moves it is also moved by something else, then it must itself be moved by something else and that (in its turn) by something else. But this cannot go on into eternity because in this way there would not be something that was first moved because the second

Boethius being comforted in dungeon by Philosophy personified (from a manuscript from the beginning of the 13th century)
The Roman philosopher, writer and statesman Boethius (c. 480–524) was one of the consuls of the Ostrogoth king Theoderic. After interceding on behalf of a friend accused of high treason, Boethius himself was also thrown into prison and executed. While in prison, he wrote his famous dialogue "De consolatione philosophiae" ("The consolation of Philosophy"), a conversation between himself and personified Philosophy, which was widely read during the Middle Ages and soon translated into Old High German by the St. Gallen monk Notker Labeo. Translations by Boethius of Aristotle's writings and of works by Porphyry were among the main sources of knowledge in the Middle Ages of Greek philosophy.

moving causes only movement because they are moved by a thing that first moved, as for example when the staff moves because it is moved by the hand. Thus it is necessary to come to something that is the first to move that is not moved by anything. And this we all understand to be God."[10]

This is the form in which other proofs of the existence of God are presented, i.e. by deducing something from a concept. It was not until the 18th century that the philosopher Immanuel Kant, in his *Critique of Pure Reason,* showed that this was not the path to take on the search for real knowledge, and why it was not. For mediaeval philosophers, this or that premise could at the most be wrong, this or that conclusion inadmissable; but as a means of reaching knowledge, speculative thought – i.e. thought deduced from concepts and developing the content of a concept and its logical associations – was out of the question.

Finally, however, it must again be stressed that the way to God, which they were all searching for, each in his own way, was not as rational for everyone as has been demonstrated here. The ordinary people, the common folk carried on living with their symbolic relationship to the world and to God without the influence of such thoughts. And the mystics, including many women, cultivated a meditative way of experiencing God, a way of which they spoke in tones of delight and enlightenment so that others would be able to share their experience of God.

Notes

1 Kühn, D.: *Der Parzival des Wolfram von Eschenbach* (Frankfurt/M., 1986).
2 Elias, N.: *Über den Prozeß der Zivilisation,* vol. 1 (Frankfurt/M., ⁵1978), p. 88.
3 Gurjewitsch, A. J.: *Das Weltbild des mittelalterlichen Menschen* (Munich, 1986), p. 102.
4 Fuhrmann, H.: *Einladung ins Mittelalter* (Munich, 1987), p. 195–236.
5 *Ibid.,* p. 200.
6 Glockner, H. (ed.): Hegel, G. W. F., *Sämtliche Werke,* vol. 19 (Stuttgart, 1928), p. 149.
7 Pieper, J.: "Scholastik." Gestalten und Probleme der mittelalterlichen Philosophie (Munich, 1960), p. 28.
8 Kluxen, W.: "Thomas von Aquin: Das Seiende und seine Prinzipien" in Speck, J. (ed.): *Grundprobleme der großen Philosophen. Philosophie des Altertums und des Mittelalters* (Göttingen, 1972), p. 182.
9 Pieper, J.: *Ibid.,* p. 160.
10 Horst Seidl (ed.): *Thomas von Aquin: Die Gottesbeweise* (Hamburg, 1982).